READING LITERATURE ALOUD

Reading Literature Aloud

LAWRENCE H. MOUAT
San Jose State College, California

New York   Oxford University Press   1962

In memory of Lee Emerson Bassett

PREFACE

In this text an attempt has been made to develop within the student an appreciation of literature as well as the desire to share that appreciation with others through effective reading aloud. The development of a complete theory of literary criticism is neither necessary nor possible, but the student is guided in selecting and assimilating worthwhile material to read aloud so that he will not be dependent on the tastes of others and so that he will obtain the maximum pleasure and benefit from what he reads.

There is a need for technique in oral reading as there is in any art form. Such technique is not an end in itself but a means of ensuring competent and complete communication of thought and feeling. I deplore the artificiality of mechanical theories of oral expression as heartily as I do the impotency of the "think the thought" school. This book is intended to furnish tools, not rules.

It is difficult to draw the line between telling the student what he should know or do and challenging him to acquire knowledge and to develop skills on his own. I hope the book has achieved a sensible middle ground. Naturally I have revealed my own preferences in selection, my own method of preparation, and my own style of interpretation as I discuss material for oral reading, but I have endeavored not to impose our way upon the student. I have tried as much as possible to encourage him to make his own decisions. The instructor is in a better position than I am to decide just how much help is needed in each case. He can consider the problems and the tastes of the individual and can give such advice and help at the proper place and time as will do the most good.

Since I encourage the student to select his own material for reading aloud, I have not included an anthology as such in the text. The selections the book does have are designed to illustrate a particular point made or, as in the lecture recitals, to exemplify a continuity of reading material. There are enough selections, however, for the student to read without going elsewhere if he is satisfied with what he finds here, or if the instructor prefers to have the class study the same material. I do hope that the student will be motivated to search for the literature that he will enjoy the most to read to himself and to others.

San Jose, California   L. H. M.
January 1962

CONTENTS

READING LITERATURE ALOUD

I

INTRODUCTION

It is surprising to discover how many occasions in our modern society call for good oral reading. In the home, parents read to children, to friends, and to each other. In the school, both teachers and students have to read aloud. At the club, minutes, letters, and announcements are read to the group. In the business and political world, reports, papers, and speeches are read. And then there are the professional readers in the pulpit, on the air, and on the stage or public platform. The growth and spread of Readers' Theatre and of reading hours, especially on the college or university campus, are indicative of interest in this kind of entertainment. For business or for pleasure, in formal or in informal situations, oral reading has a very real place in the lives of most of us.

The need for better reading

Too often the reading we hear is ineffective: the thought is broken or the feeling is lost. The meaning is obscured or missed altogether. How often have you wished that ministers would not be so sepulchral, politicians so pompous and unnatural, teachers so pedantic, business executives so tedious, actors so arty, and poets so unearthly when they read aloud? Some people read poorly through affectation, but many do so through ignorance. Such people simply don't know *how* to read aloud.

The goal of good oral reading

The "how" of reading aloud will be a major concern of this book. Here we wish to stress our prime objective, the *effective communication of all that appears on the printed page*. We communicate effectively when we speak well and we should do no less when we read aloud. Unfortunately we have often missed the early training that helps to make oral reading as effective as good

3

speaking. So although we usually speak with natural and spontaneous expression we frequently read without expression at all or strive too hard to "put expression" into our reading. Communication is hampered in either case.

In his text on public speaking Winans * insists that you will be effective in oral communication only when you have "1) a full realization of the content of your words as you utter them, and 2) a lively sense of communication." This was written to aid the public speaker in communicating his own ideas, but it applies equally well to the oral reader who wishes to communicate the ideas of another. When the public speaker is sincere and determined in his desire to say something worth while and has organized his ideas effectively, there is every likelihood that when he delivers a speech he will keep these points in mind. But in oral reading one is apt to forget. The reader becomes so engrossed with his own grasp of the material that he takes it for granted that his audience will "get it" too.

Ours is the task, then, of learning to communicate as effectively when we read aloud as we do when we speak well. We must also bear in mind that up to and including the moment of utterance we must have in mind a "lively sense of communication."

The focus on reading literature

Since the field of oral reading is so vast, it seems wise to give our attention to one area that will be of benefit to all. To confine ourselves to the purely practical—training in the reading of minutes and reports, for instance—would be as unwise as to confine ourselves to the purely professional—the preparation of programs for public performance. Let us rather give our attention to the reading of good literature aloud. If we can learn to communicate effectively the best that has been thought and expressed by others, we will have no trouble reading for both business and professional purposes, and, at the same time we will have found much to enrich our lives and the lives of those who listen to us.

It is obvious that you will neither have the time nor the inclination to read aloud everything that you have grown to like. But there is some literature that seems especially pleasing to the ear, material that is of such a nature that it is most effective when read aloud. Moreover, much that is of worth in a literary selection is

* James A. Winans, *Speech Making,* New York, 1938, p. 25.

often missed unless it is subjected to the penetrating study required for satisfactory oral reading.

Artistry in reading aloud

It is as much of an art to interpret a work of literature as it is to interpret a musical composition. Indeed the oral reader and the piano player have much in common. Each studies and develops an appreciation of the worth of the material that is recorded, in words for the one, in musical notation for the other. Each interprets the material by revealing his understanding and appreciation of it through the medium of sound. But the instruments are different; the reader uses his voice, the pianist his piano. It is an art to perform well with either.

The oral reader and the pianist differ as artists from the writer and the composer. These last are *creative;* the oral reader and the pianist are *re-creative* artists. This re-creation is not merely a mechanical process, however. True, the oral reader or pianist must be accurate. The notes and words must be presented "letter perfect," and the tempo and rhythms must be faithfully reproduced, but the instrument employed (voice or piano) is his own. The instrument reveals his own personality, his own interpretative abilities, his own artistry even as he accurately reads aloud or plays what is written by another.

Style in reading aloud

Your style of interpretation is your own, but it will be affected by the nature of the literature you interpret as well as by the intent of the author. You will be less likely to make direct contact with your listeners when you are reading the subjective, personal reflections likely to be found in sonnets, odes, and other lyrics than you will be when reading narrative material, didactic essays, sermons, or speeches. When you read dramatic literature you will probably prefer to have your listeners see the characters *in* you; while reading nondramatic material you may wish to have your listeners see the characters *through* you. If, on the other hand, you choose to dramatize a lyric, or prefer to *suggest* rather than to *become* a character in a play, your interpretation will be altogether different.

T. S. Eliot, in "The Three Voices of Poetry," * defines the

* *Atlantic Monthly,* April 1954, p. 37.

various intentions of the poet that apply equally well to the writer of prose. He says,

> The first voice is the voice of the poet talking to himself— or to nobody. The second is the voice of the poet addressing an audience, whether large or small. The third is the voice of the poet . . . when he is saying not what he would say in his own person, but only what he can say within the limits of one imaginary character addressing another imaginary character.

If you are aware of the poet's intent you will be less likely to be unjust to him in your reading. You will respect the intimacy called for in the "first voice," strive to make the desired impression on your listeners in the "second voice," and decide how you can best reveal the drama in the "third voice." Whatever may be your style of interpretation, as a re-creative artist you will be responsible for giving an accurate reproduction of all that the author has set down.

Attitudes in reading aloud

It should be clear by now that whatever else the role of the oral reader may be, it should not be that of Exhibit A. If you will permit us again to refer to the concert pianist, we could name too many who put themselves first and the music second. They attempt "brilliant" pieces so that the audience will gasp at their technique and virtuosity. The curtain call is for them and not for the music. There is no one, however, who would deny that Dame Myra Hess, for example, is an artist who loves music, whose technique is flawless but unobtrusive, who "reads" on the stage so that there can be no mistake that it is the music, not the musician, that is to be enjoyed. As we said previously, you may not read literature before a large paying audience, but whether you do or not, your concern should be with *sharing* the literature with those who are listening to you, making it live for them as it lives for you. Indeed, it may be said that, in a way, you are a *part* of the audience. You too are enjoying the selection.

Develop sound attitudes now before you start your study of reading literature aloud. Develop an attitude of respect toward your author and his work. Yours is the task of giving a faithful as well as an artistic interpretation of the selection. Develop an attitude of responsibility toward your listeners. Your task is not complete when you have mastered the material yourself nor yet when you have developed effective techniques for reading aloud. To share completely what you have come to appreciate requires a constant intent to communicate up to and including the moment of utterance. Develop an attitude of humility toward yourself. If you did not write the material you should not seek false recognition. Your reward should be the knowledge that you have shared successfully the pleasures that have been yours.

Preview

It is our intention first of all to furnish you with the basic technique needed to achieve effective oral communication in reading aloud. Then we hope to guide you in your selection, assimilation, and presentation of worth-while literary material to others.

II

BASIC TECHNIQUES

Speak the speech, I pray you, as I pronounced it to you, trippingly on the tongue: but if you mouth it, as many of your players do, I had as lief the town-crier spoke my lines. Nor do not saw the air too much with your hand, thus; but use all gently: for in the very torrent, tempest, and, as I may say, whirlwind of passion, you must acquire and beget a temperance that may give it smoothness. O, it offends me to the soul to hear a robustious periwigpated fellow tear a passion to tatters, to very rags, to split the ears of the groundlings, who for the most part are capable of nothing but inexplicable dumb-shows and noise: I would have such a fellow whipped for o'erdoing Termagant; it out-herods Herod: pray you, avoid it.

Be not too tame neither, but let your own discretion be your tutor: suit the action to the word, the word to the action; with this special observance, that you o'erstep not the modesty of nature; for anything so overdone is from the purpose of playing, whose end, both at the first and now, was and is, to hold, as 'twere, the mirror up to nature; to show virtue her own feature, scorn her own image, and the very age and body of the time his form and pressure. Now, this overdone, or come tardy off, though it make the unskilful laugh, cannot but make the judicious grieve; the censure of which one must in your allowance o'erweigh a whole theatre of others. O, there be players that I have seen play, and heard others praise, and that highly, not to speak it profanely, that neither having the accent of Christians nor the gait of Christian, pagan, nor man, have so strutted and bellowed that I have thought some of nature's journeymen had made men and not made them well, they imitated humanity so abominably.

Hamlet, III, ii.

8

Reading aloud is an art and art requires technique. To deny the existence or the importance of technique in oral reading is as unrealistic as to deny it in piano playing. To be sure, technique must not be noticed as such—"true art conceals art"—but it must be there.

A page of printed symbols is, as we have seen, the medium employed by the author to record an impression of life. However memorable his thoughts may be, they are shackled to paper with alphabetical, syntactical, and punctuational chains. He who has learned to read silently can free the living word from the printed page and enjoy what he finds there. But the living word is still a silent word, and the training you received to read silently is not adequate for effective oral reading.

The disciplines required for silent and oral reading are essentially different, because the media are different. Visual symbols, arranged spatially, are used in the one; audible symbols, transmitted temporally, are used in the other. In silent reading whole sentences and even paragraphs can be comprehended at a glance. Oral reading must follow the speaking rate. Single words and even syllables must receive attention. The printed words and the punctuation marks alone are sufficient to convey meaning to the silent reader. But when a person reads aloud, thought, mood, and feeling must be conveyed by vocal sounds; not merely by the sounds that represent the articulation and pronunciation of the words themselves but by all of the elements, variations, and nuances of voice that enter into effective oral communication. In short, the oral reader must translate, as it were, space into time and sight into sound.

If people could read aloud as easily as they speak, there would be no need to pay special attention to technique in oral reading. The nuances and variations of voice, together with accompanying bodily activity, are learned unconsciously at the time we begin to speak the language, but they often must be learned consciously when we attempt to read the literature of the language aloud. So if we can discover how certain vocal factors and bodily activities are used to facilitate the communication of thought and feeling in speaking, we will be better able to communicate successfully in oral reading.

If we fail in our task to communicate *all* that is contained on the printed page, if we merely utter words without employing the techniques necessary to make them meaningful, our listeners will lose much if not all of the author's message. The ears of the listeners are not equipped to perform the same function in hearing the words in isolation that his eyes perform in seeing the words in isolation. It is necessary for the oral reader to assist the listener in comprehending and appreciating what he hears. What then, are the techniques specifically required for oral readings?

1 VOCAL FACTORS

In describing the nature of vocal sound, voice scientists commonly list intensity, pitch, quality, and duration as its attributes. But since we feel that it is not our principal concern to deal with the problems of voice and speech improvement but rather to focus our attention on matters directly concerned with oral reading, we shall discuss also some of the subdivisions of these terms and treat them functionally rather than acoustically or physiologically. Accordingly, we will list stress, pause, pitch, quality, tempo, and intensity as the factors of voice involved in meaningful oral communication.

You will notice as we proceed that some of these vocal factors are primarily concerned with clarifying the thought and others with expressing the feeling involved. It must be understood, however, that although the intellectual and the emotional content of a selection can be studied separately, there is no actual dichotomy. Both elements are present in varying degrees in all expression. If the intellectual were missing the passage would be meaningless. If the emotional were missing the passage would be lifeless.

You will be studying basic techniques in this chapter, so that you will be able to communicate the full meaning of the printed page; but you must realize that no single technique can be employed all by itself in oral communication any more than can the intellectual content be completely separated from the emotional content of the passage read. It is only when you employ all of these techniques together, accurately and naturally, that you will truly be holding the "mirror up to nature."

a Stress

Defined as "accent," stress is a natural function of our language. In words of two or more syllables more stress, or force, is placed on one syllable than on another. This results in *primary accent* (′) e.g. re·buke′, na′ture, po·ta′to, etc. A *secondary accent*

(′) often occurs within longer words, e.g. nec′es·sar′i·ly, near′-sight′ed·ness, birth′right′, etc. Everyone is familiar with the phenomenon. Primary and secondary accent marks are shown in the dictionary.

But, in addition to the natural function of syllable accentuation, stress is directly concerned with the oral communication of meaning. We utter the *idea-carrying words* of a phrase or a sentence with more force than we give to the other words.

> I know not what course *others* may take, but as for *me,* give me *liberty* or give me *death!*

Sometimes words are stressed to distinguish between ideas.

> What is that in the *road* ahead?

is different from

> What is that in the road, a *head?*

(The comma and the spelling cannot be conveyed vocally.) This phenomenon is known as *sense stress.*

Often when a second grader reads, "Look, Jane! Look at the pretty kitty," he stresses every single syllable. He is learning his words and wants himself and everyone else to know it. Then one occasionally hears a fourth grader reading aloud stressing nothing at all and reading everything in a deadening monotone. He knows the words, assumes that we do too, and is interested solely in getting to the end of what he is reading. In both cases the listener will get but little meaning out of the "reading" unless he makes a special effort to "translate" the lines into intelligible phrases using his "mind's ear" to put the sense stress where it belongs.

Too many of us, unfortunately, when reading aloud never get much beyond the level of these elementary school pupils. We read words and words only, monotonously, or in a sing-song pattern, probably getting but a modicum of the thought content ourselves and certainly giving very little of it to anyone else. True, we are not all as bad as the youthful beginner, but to the extent that we fail to emphasize the idea-carrying words—to the extent, that is, that we omit the sense stress—we fail to clarify the thought.

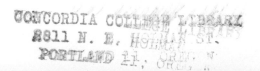

Sense stress usually coincides with the accent on a polysyllabic word, so that, technically, the entire word is not stressed, but only the accented syllable:

'Tis the very *witch*ing time of night.

Genius is *one*-tenth *in*spiration and *nine*-tenths *per*spiration.

In certain cases, however, sense stress deliberately changes the natural accent of words:

The *as*cent was bad en*ough,* but the *de*scent was ap*pall*ing.

You pronounce the word "hun*dred*" not "hun*derd.*"

Idea-carrying words are not fixed. They cannot be listed. The same sentence may convey a number of completely different meanings depending on which is, in fact, the idea-carrying word (or words). Here is a common expression that is a good illustration.

I'm glad you're here this evening. (Even though nobody else is.)

I'm *glad* you're here this evening. (Did you think I was disappointed?)

I'm glad *you're* here this evening. (These other people frankly bore me, though.)

I'm glad you're *here* this evening. (It's so reassuring to see you, right here.)

I'm glad you're here *this* evening. (If you were here last evening I would not have seen you.)

I'm glad you're here this *eve*ning. (It's much too hot any other time of the day.)

And, of course, if you stressed two words instead of one, the meaning would be still different.

I'm glad you're *here* this evening, or

I'm *glad* you're here *this* evening, etc.

In this illustration it is presumed that you know the exact meaning and have only to stress the idea-carrying words to convey that meaning to others. Often, however, you will encounter in your reading a passage that permits more than one interpretation. Even after careful study you may discover that a choice must be made. What *are* the idea-carrying words to be stressed? Consider, for instance, the first line of the famous 23rd Psalm:

The Lord is my Shepherd, I shall not want.

If "Lord" and "my" are stressed, it would imply that other people may prefer different shepherds. If "Shepherd" is stressed, it could indicate that the Lord is regarded as a protector rather than a tyrant. Similarly, if "I" is stressed, the thought may be conveyed that other people may be unhappy but not I; whereas if "want" is stressed, the assurance of being provided for is the essence of the meaning. So one person may read the sentence this way:

The *Lord* is *my* Shepherd, *I* shall not want.

and another may read this way:

The Lord is my *Shep*herd, I shall not *want.*

How would you read it?

The last line from Amy Lowell's "Patterns" presents a similar difficulty. You must read the poem, of course, to appreciate the problem. This is the line:

Christ! What are patterns for?

The whole line might be considered a blasphemy. If this is the essence of the thought, then only *Christ* is stressed. But, if in addition to calling upon the deity, one honestly searches for an answer, then "for" is stressed. Again, one may be inveighing against the inevitable appearance of patterns in the nature of things. The word "patterns" would be stressed then. If one really wants to know the answer to the question, "are" could be stressed. Finally, which seems unlikely, if one is speaking most confidentially, intimately, and dispassionately to Christ Himself, he might stress "what." All these interpretations are possible. But which one fits?

In Hamlet's advice to the players (p. 8) we read:

> ". . . anything so overdone is from the purpose of playing. . ."

Which word do you stress, "from" or "playing"? And, again,

> ". . . the censure of which one must in your opinion o'erweigh a whole theatre of others."

Do you stress "one" or "must"? In each of these two examples there is only one right answer—which is called for by the context. What are the right answers?

From the preceding analysis we can see how basic the factor of stress is in clarifying thought in oral communication. When one is speaking with conviction and fluency, he stresses unerringly, indeed unconsciously. But when he reads aloud, he is not so apt to stress properly, unless he gives his attention to the need for sense stress.

Stress the words that carry the meaning. Do it naturally. Do it as you do when speaking effectively. More than any other single factor, sense stress, when properly utilized, clarifies the thought and achieves that degree of naturalness that makes for effective oral communication.

Here are a number of lines for you to practice on. First of all, get the meaning yourself, and be sure you have it. It might be well to paraphrase the ideas in your own words. Next, underline the accented syllable of the idea-carrying words, the words you feel should be stressed when you read the lines aloud. It is essential that you discover these words by hearing them—not by looking at them. Always remember that oral reading should be just as natural as good speaking. So *speak* the lines in order to discover the natural sense stress. There may be more than one set of words that carry the sense stress, but be prepared to justify the set that you decide upon.

Every why hath a wherefore.

We know what we are, but we know not what we may be.

A great memory does not make a philosopher, any more than a dictionary can be called a grammar.

They are as sick that surfeit with too much as they that starve with nothing.

Some are born great, some achieve greatness, and some have greatness thrust upon them.

Men's evil manners live in brass; their virtues we write in water.

The conformation of his mind was such that whatever was little seemed to him great, and whatever was great seemed to him little.

The hearing ear is always found close to the speaking tongue.

He knows not when to be silent who knows not when to speak.

Cato said, "I had rather men should ask why my statue is not set up, than why it is."

I am a man, and nothing that concerns a man do I deem a matter of indifference to me.

And a woman is only a woman, but a good cigar is a smoke.

There is no heroic poem in the world but is at bottom a biography, the life of a man; also, it may be said, there is no life of a man, faithfully recorded, but is a heroic poem of its sort, rhymed or unrhymed.

She swore, in faith, 'twas strange.

Might and reason exist on different planes, and force never disproves truth.

b Pause

We express thought and feeling by the pause *between* words as well as by the stress *upon* words.

We have to pause once in a while in any oral communication or we would soon run out of breath. It is highly desirable that pausing for breathing correspond with pausing for meaning. Such pausing is made automatically in speaking, unless we are breathless from exertion or from some emotional disturbance, but it has to be learned in oral reading. The printed page does not furnish us with adequate clues.

For one thing, although words are separated one from the other in print, we do not pause between every single word in speech any more than we pause between every single syllable.

How are you, today?

It's all the same to me.

The lady doth protest too much, methinks.

exemplify this continuity. Rather do we pause between *thought groups,* groups representing units of meaning. We are accustomed to such thought groups as the paragraph and the sentence, where we always pause, and the clause and the phrase, where we frequently pause. But, in a sense, the subject of a sentence is a thought separate from the predicate, and each member of a compound subject or predicate is a separate thought. It is not at all unusual in normal speech to pause between such groups. In the sentence

The most priceless possession that a teacher can have is the knowledge that he has instilled the love of wisdom in the heart of a pupil.

one might well pause after "have."
And in the sentence

There is so little good in the best of us and so little bad in the worst of us that it ill behooves the most of us to speak about the rest of us.

one might pause after each "us."

The punctuation marks of the printed page cannot be relied upon entirely as guides to pause. We usually pause at periods, colons, and even semicolons, but we do not always pause at commas, and, what is more to the point, we often pause where there are *no* commas. In the expression

Yes, sir.

we do not pause at the comma; nor do we pause at the first comma (in normal speech) in the sentence

It has often been suggested that, since true art consists of interpreting nature, naturalism is not true art.

And in the sentence

To say nothing wisely is as abortive as to utter profound truths crudely.

we might pause after "wisely," where there is no comma. Or in the epigram

He who can does; he who can't teaches; and he who can't teach preaches.

we would most likely pause at the semicolons but, in addition, we could pause after "can," "can't," and "teach."

The point of the matter is this: punctuation marks are syntactical devices; they indicate grammatical relationships. The pause (together with other vocal factors) is a psychological device: it indicates thought relationships. The two devices frequently coincide, but not always.

Mark, if you will, the selections that follow with vertical lines at places where you feel significant pauses are in order. Be guided but not misled by punctuation marks, and consider pausing where there are no punctuation marks. As in the last section where idea-carrying words were to be underlined for stress, a choice is frequently possible. But, as with stress, while there may be more than one right way, there may be wrong ways. So determine your thought groupings carefully. Use your ear as well as your eye as you focus on this assignment. Then be sure you can justify the grouping you create. Read the passages aloud to yourself and to others. Are your pauses located where they would be if you were communicating meaningfully in normal speech? You might indicate the sense stress too, by underlining the accented syllables of the idea-carrying words.

> He who knows not and knows not that he knows not is a fool; shun him.
> He who knows not and knows that he knows not is a child; teach him.
> He who knows and knows not that he knows is asleep; wake him.
> He who knows and knows that he knows is a wise man; follow him.

> Next to the originator of a good sentence is the first quoter of it.

> [He is] a sophisticated rhetorician, inebriated with the exuberance of his own verbosity, and gifted with an egotistical imagination that can at all times command an interminable and inconsistent series of arguments to malign an opponent and to glorify himself.

> I repeat . . . that all power is a trust; that we are accountable for its exercise; that from the people and for the people all springs, and all must exist.

In the opinion of fools teaching is a humble task, but in fact it is the noblest of occupations.

Put out the light, and then put out the light.

Books must follow sciences, and not sciences books. [Don't make us ask: "What kind of 'books' are 'sciences books'?"]

The world is a comedy to those that think, a tragedy to those who feel.

In giving freedom to the slave we assure freedom to the free, honorable alike in what we give and what we preserve.

Supper was over, and the process of digestion proceeding as favorably as, under the influence of complete tranquility and cheerful conversation, most wise men conversant with the anatomy and functions of the human frame will consider that it ought to have proceeded, when the three friends were startled by the noise of loud and angry threatenings below stairs.

We pause on occasion to enhance the meaning as well as to clarify it. When we wish to impress, to highlight an effect, or to command a considerable degree of attention, we will often pause before a particularly significant word or we will even pause in the midst of an otherwise unbroken thought group. We might call this a *pause for effect*. Consider the last lines from the famous epistle of St. Paul to the Corinthians:

And now there remain faith, hope and love, these three; but the greatest of these is love.

A pause before the last two words just quoted does much to enhance the sublimity of the thought. Consider this passage from R. L. Stevenson's *The Lantern Bearers:*

There is a fable that touches very near to the quick of life, the fable of the monk who passed into the woods, heard a bird break into song, hearkened for a trill or two and found himself on his return a stranger at his convent gate, for he had been absent fifty years and only one remained who knew him. Life that is anything more than merely mechanical is made up of two strands, seeking for that bird and hearing him.

Would it not be delightful to pause momentarily just before the last two words, so that you and those listening to you might suspend yourselves in time (as the monk did) while the implications of the fable become clear?

c Pitch

Our voices are constantly fluctuating up and down in pitch as we talk. Such pitch variation is characteristic of a language pattern. Indeed we are frequently able to guess the nationality of the speaker by his pitch variation even though he is speaking in English and produces his speech sounds with absolute accuracy.

There appears to be a close connection between pitch change and meaning. In fact, so important is pitch change as an indication of meaning that it is frequently possible to grasp the thought by the pitch patterns alone even when the words themselves are not recognizable. For example, affirmation or assent, on occasion, is indicated by "m . . . m" with a rise in pitch on the second sound, and negation can be similarly conveyed by "m . . . m" with a fall in pitch on the second sound. Again, "What?" can be expressed by "mmm" accompanied by a gliding upward pitch. And, "I don't know" can be expressed by "mmm" with a sharp rise in pitch on the middle element above the other two. Such substitutes for conventional speech are not recommended, but they are made, and they do reflect the importance of pitch change as a factor in clarifying the thought.

Pitch change accompanies sense stress in the emphasis of idea-carrying words. Just as there is an added prominence (sense stress) given to such words over and above any natural accent, so there is an abrupt rise or fall in pitch at these same words over and above the natural fluctuation in pitch as we speak or read aloud. Read the line

I'm glad you're here this evening

stressing a different word each time according to the shift in the meaning, and you will notice that the voice goes up on the stressed word and falls immediately thereafter. When "evening" is stressed the pitch falls on the second syllable. Practice reading the exercises in the preceding sections, emphasizing the idea-carrying words again. You will notice in each case that there will be a distinct change of pitch wherever there is a distinct sense stress. The two elements are closely related.

In addition to the function of emphasizing the idea-carrying words, pitch change serves to clarify thought by separating the subordinate or the parenthetical expressions from the rest of the sentence. The main thought will follow one rather distinctive pitch level while the subordinate thought will follow another. To ensure the continuity of the main thought the voice should pick up the same pitch level *after* the subordinate expression that was employed *before* it. One might call this a sort of "pitch bridge." There should be approximately the same level at each end. For instance, in the poem "Opportunity" by Sill,

> This I beheld, or dreamed it in a dream;
> There spread a cloud of dust along a plain.
> And underneath the cloud or in it, raged
> A furious battle.

"Or dreamed it in a dream" and "or in it" are subordinate. How should they be read? There is a long pitch bridge in the passage quoted from the *Pickwick Papers* (page 19, "Supper was over . . ."). Can you "cross" it normally and easily so that the main and the subordinate thoughts will be clear and intelligible?

Pitch variation expresses feeling and mood as well as it clarifies the thought. There is more variation of pitch in light and frivolous material and less variation in heavy and somber material. A Thurber story, for instance, is read with considerably more pitch variation than the Gettysburg Address. There are obvious exceptions. A tragic line can be read with an extensive range of pitch, a comic line with little or none; but in general, the tendency just described holds true. For instance:

> What next befell me then and there
> I know not well—I never knew;

First came the loss of light, and air,
And then of darkness too;
I had no thought, no feeling—none;
Among the stones I stood a stone,
And was, scarce conscious what I wist,
As shrubless crags within the mist;
For all was blank, and bleak, and gray;
It was not night, it was not day;
It was not even the dungeon-light,
So hateful to my heavy sight,
But vacancy absorbing space,
And fixedness—without a place;
There were no stars, no earth, no time,
No check, no change, no good, no crime—
But silence, and a stirless breath
Which neither was a life nor death;
A sea of stagnant idleness,
Blind, boundless, mute, and motionless!

(BYRON, *The Prisoner of Chillon*)

would probably be read with a minimum of pitch variation, whereas

The Owl and the Pussy Cat went to sea
In a beautiful pea green boat;
They took some honey, and plenty of money
Wrapped up in a five pound note.
The Owl looked up to the stars above
And sang to a small guitar,
"O lovely Pussy, O Pussy my love,
What a beautiful Pussy you are,
        You are,
            You are,
What a beautiful Pussy you are!

(EDWARD LEAR)

would vary considerably in pitch. If you are in any doubt of this, reverse the suggestions just made for the two readings. Feeling will be expressed, but not that intended by the authors!

Before we leave the study of pitch as a vocal factor of interpretation it is interesting (but not essential) to consider the direction of pitch change—rising, falling, or both, and the nature of pitch change—by step or by glide.

We are accustomed to associating rising inflection with question marks and falling inflection with periods; but this is not necessarily so. Actually, the rise or fall of the voice is related to the completeness or the definiteness of the thought expressed. Pitch will rise where the thought is indefinite or incomplete, and will fall when the reverse is true.

In questions where a definite answer is expected, the pitch will fall after the last stressed syllable in the thought group. Such questions usually begin with an interrogative word. In linguistic terminology they are called *special questions*. Try reading the following aloud:

When shall we meet again?

Who would do a thing like that?

Where are you?

In questions where the answer is indefinite or uncertain, that is, questions that can be answered by *either* yes or no, the pitch will usually rise after the last stressed syllable in the thought group. These are technically known as *general questions*.

Have you changed your mind?

Are you afraid?

Did you call me a while ago?

Of course, the reverse direction will be followed if the intent is altered. Ask the first set of questions as though you were quite uncertain as to what the answer might be and each will end with a rising inflection. Ask the second set as though the answer were a foregone conclusion, and each will end with a falling inflection.

Short statements expressing comfort or reassurance often end with a rising inflection.

I shall not want.

That's all right.

There is a suggestion of incompleteness in such a rise in pitch. General questions are implied in each: "Shall I?" in the first, and "Isn't it?" in the second.

In longer periodic sentences containing a series of thought groups, the meaning of the whole not being completed until the very end, the voice will generally fall at the idea-carrying words in each thought group, rise again at the end of that thought group, and fall finally at the end of the last thought group.

Some are born great, some achieve greatness, and others have greatness thrust upon them.

We, the People of the United States in order to form a more perfect Union, establish Justice, insure domestic tranquility, provide for the common welfare, and secure the blessings of liberty to ourselves and our posterity, do ordain and establish this Constitution for the United States of America.

(Preamble)

Pitch change occurs either as a glide or as a distinct and discrete step. The voice will glide if the stressed syllable is final in a thought group, and it will step if the stressed syllable is not final. For example, there are two thoughts in this line:

It blesseth him that *gives* and him that *takes*.

In each thought the stressed syllable is final. The pitch change on "gives" and "takes" will be gliding (although in different directions). In these lines

With my cross-bow, I shot the albatross.

and

We are such stuff as dreams are made on,

if "shot" and "dreams" are stressed, the voice, after rising on each, will drop a definite step to the syllable following them.*

The direction and the nature of pitch change cannot easily be relegated to rules, nor is it necessary to do so. Our sole purpose is to bring to your attention the importance of pitch as a vocal factor of interpretation that is indispensable to clarity of thought and expression of feeling. We have described what happens to the pitch of the voice when one is communicating effectively with others, orally. Strive continually to make adequate use of this factor when you read aloud.

d Quality

People (and animals) are sensitive to the quality of the voice. We do not have to overhear words of courting to appraise the mood of the couple participating in the conversation. Similarly, parents can recognize the mood of their children talking vigorously in another room when the words are rendered unintelligible by the churning of the washing machine or the background blare of radio or television. Teasing, fighting, good nature, or mischief plotting are easily distinguishable. We can detect the trivial or the serious import of a one-sided telephone conversation. In short, the quality of the normal voice is an accurate barometer of feeling. The quality of voice used to reflect feeling may be referred to as a *feeling tone*.

Feeling tones are numberless. The tone may be harsh, strident, sonorous, mellow, crisp, breathy, ominous, sad, cheerful, pathetic, depending upon the feeling involved. No two of us can convey the same feeling in the same way, but if we are aware of and can control our voices in the portrayal of a particular feeling it will be recognized by others. Such feelings as excitement, joy, sorrow, hope, despair, uncertainty, anger, sympathy, scorn, fear,

* Kenneth I. Pike, *The Intonation of American English*, Ann Arbor, Univ. of Michigan Press, 1945, presents a scholarly study of pitch variation in extreme detail. It contains an extensive bibliography as well.

mirth, and many others can be expressed by suitable feeling tones. The completeness of the list of feeling tones and feelings is not so important as the awareness of their almost endless ramification.

There is no one feeling tone to accompany each single feeling or emotion, but the tone that is produced should convey the feeling intended. Each of the following expressions contains one or more definite feelings which can be revealed by the quality of the voice. What are the feelings? What tones will reveal them best?

You interest me.

This is it.

I never thought you would stoop so low!

> The quality of mercy is not strained,
> It droppeth as the gentle rain from heaven
> Upon the place beneath.

> Why so pale and wan young lover,
> Prithee why so pale?
> Will when looking well can't win her
> Looking ill prevail?
> Prithee why so pale?

With malice toward none; with charity for all; with firmness in the right as God gives us to see the right, let us strive on to finish the work we are in; to bind up the nation's wounds, to care for him who shall have borne the battle, and for his widow and orphans—to do all which may achieve and cherish a just and lasting peace among ourselves and with all nations.

> Hang out our banners on the outward walls.
> The cry is still, "They come"; our castle's strength
> Will laugh a siege to scorn; here let them lie
> Till famine and the ague eat them up.

Don't quibble, Sybil.

It is my living sentiment, and by the blessing of God it shall be my dying sentiment—Independence now and Independence forever!

Going my way, soldier?

It might be interesting to take one single word to see how many possible feeling tones it can reflect in conformance to the meaning. Take the word "well," for instance. See whether you can produce a feeling tone that will suggest these different states of mind.

doubt	condescension
contempt	confusion
surprise	remonstrance
indignation	decision
love	coquetry

If you can manage so to adjust your voice that its quality can suggest every shade of feeling, every overtone of mood, and every nuance of meaning that may be contained within a selection of literary worth; then you will have come close indeed to a full realization of your potentialities as an oral reader of literature. Can you reveal the dominant mood or feeling contained in each of the following selections by producing the proper feeling tone?

Dreamy

> In the afternoon they came unto a land
> In which it seemed always afternoon.
> All round the coast the languid air did swoon,
> Breathing like one that hath a weary dream.
> Full-faced above the valley stood the moon;
> And like a downward smoke, the slender stream
> Along the cliff to fall and pause and fall did seem.
>
> (TENNYSON, *"The Lotos-Eaters"*)

Solemn

We hold these truths to be self-evident: that all men are created equal and are endowed by their Creator with certain unalienable rights, and that among these are life, liberty, and the pursuit of happiness.

(Preamble to the Declaration of Independence)

Fascinating

Whenas in silks my Julia goes,
Then, then, methinks, how sweetly flows
The liquefaction of her clothes!

Next when I cast mine eyes and see
That brave vibration each way free,
—O how that glittering taketh me!

(HERRICK, *Upon Julia's Clothes*)

Pathetic

She lived unknown, and few could know
When Lucy ceased to be;
But she is in her grave, and oh,
The difference to me!

(WORDSWORTH, *Lucy*)

Hilarious

They went to sea in a sieve they did;
In a sieve they went to sea:
In spite of all their friends could say,
On a winter's morn and a stormy day,
In a sieve they went to sea.
And when the sieve turned round and round
And everyone cried, "You'll all be drowned!"
They called aloud, "Our sieve ain't big;
But we don't care a button, we don't care a fig;
In a sieve we'll go to sea!"

(LEAR, *The Jumblies*)

Horrible

Skymaster lurched again, very sharply. The young man writing to Mom looked up . . . I was holding up another piece
of paper and looked around it at the baby. My eye was just
around the edge. Suddenly, so suddenly I still do not know
what happened, my backbone felt as if it had been shot
through the top of my head. I saw two blue eyes. They hit
a steel rod. A child's head was bloody. I had no breath.
Then all was black.

(DOROTHY KAUCHER, *On Your Left the Milky Way*)

Determined

We shall not flag nor fail. We shall go on to the end. We
shall fight in France and on the seas and oceans; we shall
fight with growing confidence and growing strength in the
air. We shall defend our island whatever the cost may be;
we shall fight on beaches, landing grounds, in fields, in streets,
and on the hills. We shall never surrender, and even if, which
I do not for a moment believe, this island or a large part of
it were subjugated and starving, then our empire beyond the
seas, armed and guarded by the British Fleet, will carry on
the struggle until in God's good time the New World, with
all its power and might, sets forth to the liberation and
rescue of the Old.

(WINSTON CHURCHILL)

e Tempo

The tempo of speech is the rate or speed of utterance. The
range is considerable. Some ponderously slow speakers utter as
few as 80 words a minute, the rapid fire speaker 180 words. The
average speaking rate is between 110 and 120 words a minute.
When you read the speeches or lines of another, adjust the tempo
to his personality and to his mood.

Tempo reflects feeling and mood. The unimportant is usually

expressed more rapidly than the important; the light, the gay, the frivolous are expressed with more speed than the heavy, the melancholy, and the serious.

> O, then I see Queen Mab hath been with you.
> She is the fairies' midwife, and she comes
> In shape no bigger than an agate stone
> On the forefinger of an alderman,
> Drawn with a team of little atomies
> Athwart men's noses as they lie asleep.
>
> *(Romeo and Juliet)*

is uttered much more rapidly than

> Tomorrow and tomorrow and tomorrow
> Creeps in this petty pace from day to day
> To the last syllable of recorded time,
> And all our yesterdays have lighted fools
> The way to dusty death.
>
> *(Macbeth)*

while

> O eloquent, just and mighty death! Whom none could advise, thou hast persuaded. What none hath dared, thou hast done. And whom all the world flattered, thou only hast cast out of the world and despised. Thou hast drawn together all the far stretched greatness, all the pride, cruelty and ambition of man, and covered it over with these two narrow words, *Hic jacet!*
>
> *(Sir Walter Raleigh)*

has an average tempo less rapid than

> Gratiano speaks an infinite deal of nothing, more than any man in all Venice. His reasons are as two grains of wheat hid in two bushels of chaff. You shall seek all day ere you

find them, and when you have them, they are not worth the search.

(*Merchant of Venice*)

There is a tempo for continuous utterance reflecting the personality of a character or the import of the lines. There is also a tempo, or, more precisely, a *duration,* for the utterance of individual words. In some selections we find a preponderance of long full vowels, where, for instance, languor, melancholy, or dignity prevail. If we linger on these sounds stretching them out, so to speak, in duration, we will not only reveal the full meaning more completely but we will enhance the language chosen by the author, or the sequence of sounds deliberately devised to secure the effect desired.

Notice the length of consecutive vowel sounds in the Psalms, in the Gettysburg Address, and in all sad, solemn, impressive utterances.

> Sunset and evening star,
>> And one clear call for me!
> And may there be no moaning of the bar,
>> When I put out to sea,
>
> But such a tide as moving seems asleep,
>> Too full for sound and foam,
> When that which drew from out the boundless deep
>> Turns again home.
>
> Twilight and evening bell,
>> And after that the dark!
> And may there be no sadness of farewell,
>> When I embark;
>
> For tho' from out our bourne of Time and Place
>> The flood may bear me far,
> I hope to see my Pilot face to face
>> When I have crost the bar.

(TENNYSON, *Crossing the Bar*)

and

It was night, and the rain fell; and, falling, it was rain, but having fallen, it was blood. And I stood in the morass among the tall lilies, and the rain fell upon my head—and the lilies sighed one unto the other in the solemnity of their desolation.

And, all at once, the moon arose through the thin ghastly mist, and was crimson in color. And mine eyes fell upon a huge gray rock which stood by the shore of the river, and was lighted by the light of the moon. And the rock was gray, and ghastly, and tall—and the rock was gray. Upon its front were characters engraven in the stone; and I walked through the morass of water-lilies, until I came close unto the shore, that I might read the characters upon the stone. But I could not decipher them. And I was going back into the morass, when the moon shone with a fuller red, and I turned and looked again upon the rock, and upon the characters, and the characters were *Desolation*.

And I looked upward, and there stood a man upon the summit of the rock; and I hid myself among the water-lilies that I might discover the actions of the man. And the man was tall and stately in form, and was wrapped up from his shoulders to his feet in the toga of old Rome. And the outlines of his figure were indistinct—but his features were the features of a deity; for the mantle of the night, and of the mist, and of the moon, and of the dew, had left uncovered the features of his face. And his brow was lofty with thought, and his eye wild with care; and, in the few furrows upon his cheek I read the fables of sorrow, and weariness, and disgust with mankind, and a longing after solitude.

And the man sat upon the rock, and leaned his head upon his hand, and looked out upon the desolation. He looked down into the low, unquiet shrubbery, and up into the tall primeval trees, and up higher at the rustling heaven, and into the crimson moon. And I lay close within the shelter of the lilies, and observed the actions of the man. And the man trembled in the solitude—but the night waned, and he sat upon the rock.

(POE, *Silence—A Fable*)

In other selections we find a preponderance of short, "choppy" vowels. They appear particularly in gay, light, humorous material and in passages of unimportant descriptive detail.

Notice this effect in the following:

I am the very model of a modern major-general,
I've information vegetable, animal, and mineral;
I know the Kings of England, and I quote the fights historical,
From Marathon to Waterloo, in order categorical;
I'm very well acquainted too, with matters mathematical,
I understand equations, both the simple and quadratical;
About binomial theorem I'm teeming with a lot o'news,
With interesting facts about the square of the hypotenuse,
I'm very good at integral and differential calculus,
I know the scientific names of beings animalculous,
In short, in matters vegetable, animal and mineral,
I am the very model of a modern major-general.

(W. S. GILBERT, *The Pirates of Penzance*)

or, in these airplane impressions:

We leaped a cloud. Plop! Plop! Plop! Stern jaws of the California coast range thrust their hard lines skyward beneath us. Bellowing purple cloud banks bowed like very proper skywalkers.

"Be calm, Zelda. Be calm!"

That is what Uncle Henry always called to Aunt Zelda when a cyclone propelled both of them over the cowshed in northwest Missouri and they had exchanged false teeth in the scrambling exit.

(KAUCHER, *On Your Left the Milky Way*)

f Intensity

Intensity of speech is the degree of energy exerted. It does not necessarily produce loudness, although loudness is a function of intensity.* It is quite possible to exert a great deal of energy and yet speak in a voice a little above a whisper. Shylock, in anger, might well have spoken the lines;

> How like a fawning publican he looks! I hate him, for he is a Christian. But more for that, in low simplicity he lends out money gratis and brings down the rate of usance here with us in Venice. If I can catch him once upon the hip, I will feed fat the ancient grudge I bear him.

with considerable venom and energy yet in a voice scarcely above a whisper. But

> If I were an American as I am an Englishman, while a foreign troop were landed on my shore, I would never lay down my arms. Never! Never! Never!

could hardly be expressed without rafter splintering loudness.

Ordinarily the loudness (and simultaneously the pitch frequency) of our voice increases when we are angry, vehement, excited, or forceful. We speak in softer, quieter tones when we are calm, depressed, restful, or dignified. But whether an increase in loudness does or does not accompany an increase in the intensity of vocal utterance, it is apparent that if this vocal factor so definitely reflects our mood and feeling in self-expression, it must be employed in a similar way when we express the thoughts of others.

Intensity is a factor most helpful in enhancing the effect of certain sound sequences. A sequence of words containing like initial sounds, consonants or vowels, produces *alliteration*. An

---

* Technically, *stress* is closely akin to loudness, inasmuch as accented syllables are uttered with more loudness than unaccented syllables. But, in this section we are concerned with the loudness employed on an entire passage or sequence. One would still stress the accented syllables or the idea-carrying words with more force (loudness) than would be given to the passage as a whole.

added intensity to such a sequence will reveal the pure pleasure found in the sounds themselves. An excellent example:

> The fair breeze blew, the white foam flew,
> The furrow followed free;
> We were the first that ever burst
> Into that silent sea.

Rhyming vowel sounds in the accented syllable followed by unlike consonant sounds is called *assonance*. In the following extract from Tennyson's "Passing of Arthur," assonance is noticeable particularly in the third and fourth lines. Alliteration is present too. Can you do justice to these effects in reading the passage aloud?

> And ever and anon with host to host
> Shocks, and the splintering spear, the hard mail hewn
> Shield breaking, and the clash of brands, the crash
> Of battle axes on shattered helms, and shrieks
> After the Christ of those, falling down,
> Look'd up for heaven, and only saw the mist.

As you study the material you select for oral interpretation, watch for the effects we have just described. If the sounds and sound sequences are pleasing to you it is because the style is right, the form is artistic. The suggestions we have just offered for utilizing various vocal factors in interpretation, especially those directly concerned with expressing mood and feeling (quality, tempo, and intensity), will enable you to re-create the impressions for others.

2 BODY BEHAVIOR

There are no set rules for body behavior any more than there are for vocal manipulations. Time was when the student was taught that there was a muscular movement to correspond with each thought or feeling, and charts were prepared to indicate the appropriate action. Fortunately, this practice has been discouraged. But just as the voice responds to the material read, so does the rest of the body. The response will be right if the grasp of the material is complete and if the attitude toward author, self, and audience is true, particularly if the reader has a full realization of the content of his reading at the time of utterance and "a lively sense of communication." Here we shall describe *what* body behavior takes place when there is true communication, rather than suggest *how* proper body behavior should be accomplished.

In the first place when you do communicate effectively, orally, in reading as in speaking, you communicate with your total person, not just your mouth. Your entire body musculature is involved in transmitting the thought and feeling of your selection to your listeners. Sometimes this is revealed in facial expression, in posture, and even in a gesture, though, with book in hand this last would be distracting unless used most sparingly. But even when there is no visible behavior, your body tensions must be commensurate with the energy you are exerting. Indeed if you have attempted a selection of some length that is both intricate in pattern and highly emotional in content, you may very well be physically exhausted when you have finished, even though you have read quietly and with little or no visible body movement. In short, "suit the action to the word and the word to the action," realizing that, for the most part, in oral reading this action may not involve much locomotion.

Unless you are acting or impersonating or participating in a staged reading you should not be overly concerned with locomotion. Usually the interpreter is confined to a limited area and to limited movement. Occasionally, you *may* wish to move from one side of the platform or reading area to the other in order to give another part of your audience a chance for closer contact with you or to indicate that you have finished with one major mood or thought and are going on to another. When you do move for such reasons, be sure that here too, as in the case of gestures, you are not distracting. Your audience wants to hear what you read rather than to watch your physical maneuvers.

The chances are you will have a reading stand, but don't count on it. There may not be one; and, if there is, and it is not adjustable, it may be too low or too high. If there is no stand, simply read with book or script in hand. You may not need book or script, for if you have prepared well you will have made the words of your reading so nearly your own that they are memorized for practical purposes, but it is fitting that you should have it. With book in hand you establish the fact that you are sharing it with your listeners and not exhibiting yourself. If possible, hold the book in your left hand and turn the pages with your right so as not to block off your vision. If you have a script you may wish to bind it between stiff covers so that you can hold it like a book. Loose pages are distracting.

On occasion you may decide to sit rather than to stand, especially if you wish to suggest informality, restfulness, or intimacy with your audience; but if you do you must realize from what we have said about the total body response involved in a reading that you may be handicapped in the full utilization of your voice. It requires considerable effort to be effective while seated.

Look at your audience when it is helpful to do so. Look away from them or past them when it seems better that way. If you recall the "three voices of poetry" in the Introduction you will understand that the reflective, personal, intimate material of the "first voice" does not call for direct eye contact. Elizabeth Barrett Browning's "How Do I Love Thee" should not be addressed carelessly and directly to a member of the opposite sex in the audience. But material of the "second voice," direct appeal to an audience or simple narration, does call for eye contact, so be sufficiently prepared that you can make it freely.

The "third voice," in a dramatic reading, involves one imaginary character talking to another. This will appear in dialogue in stories as well as in plays. Here there should be no eye contact with the audience. A consistent turn of the head for one character, back again for a second, and a still different turn for a third, etc., or the dropping back of a foot, if you are not behind a stand, are all that is required, usually, for character differentiation. (A word may be intruded here about the use of voice in dialogue. It is important to establish a vocal pattern compatible with each character and to maintain it consistently. In distinguishing between male and female it is better to suggest the difference with a slightly lower pitch and slightly stronger muscle tone for the male, than it is to resort to falsetto or to cavernous tones.)

The main point to keep in mind is this: oral reading of literature is for enjoyment. If your attitude is really one of a "lively sense of communication" your body activity will be natural. Furthermore, you will look natural if you feel that way.

III

SELECTION OF MATERIAL

Think of life as a vast picture gallery, or museum, or better, perhaps as a vast engineering workshop. It is all those things among others. Then think of oneself walking through it. You know how the average man walks through a museum or workshop when he knows nothing particular about it. You try hard to be intelligent; failing in that you try to conceal your lack of intelligence. You would like to be interested; but you do not know what is interesting and what is not. Some of the specimens strike you as pretty; some of the engines seem to you very powerful; you are dazzled and amused by the blaze of the fires; you are secretly interested in the men and wish you could talk to them. But in the main you come out at the other end tired and rather dispirited and having got remarkably little out of it. That is the way a stupid and uneducated man, with no one to help him, goes through life.

GILBERT MURRAY

Why do we choose a particular selection to read aloud? Is it because we find it at hand, in some standard text, anthology, or collection? Is it because someone has suggested it to us, because we are already familiar with it, or because it is the right length? Or is it simply because, having read it, we like it? Most likely we will read aloud best what we enjoy the most. Certainly we should take pleasure in what we read, and we will want to share our pleasure with others when we read aloud, but how can we be sure that we have chosen something *worth* reading? How can we be sure of the value of the selection for which, presumably, we will have paid so much in time and effort?

It is our purpose here to guide you in your choice of selection, so that when you explore a book store or a library or even a collection or an anthology, you will find what you want, be aware of its worth, and be satisfied with your choice, and so that you will not come out "tired and dispirited and having got remarkably little out of it."

1 THE SEARCH FOR CRITERIA

What might you look for first when you search for literary material of worth? Suppose you were making a purchase of books, and you had a limited budget and limited space. Would not your first objective be to select that which has *lasting value,* durability, something that you would want to read again and again? Your safest bet, of course, would be to purchase books that have stood the test of time: the Bible, Plato, Milton, Dickens, Emerson, Hans Christian Andersen, Lewis Carroll, to name but a few, and, probably by now, such works as those of H. H. Munro (Saki), Somerset Maugham, and Thomas Wolfe. If you wish an anthology of poetry you might choose *The Oxford Book of English Verse,* for instance.

You would exercise the same care if you were collecting records or paintings. The music lover does not hesitate to purchase a Bach fugue or a Mozart symphony or even a "modern" classic like Gershwin, for these works will last; they can be enjoyed again and again. The lover of painting does not hesitate to buy a good Raphael or Holbein print, and he may even be captivated by Grant Wood's *American Gothic* or *Honorary Degree.* These all permit repeated scrutiny.

So if you were buying books, records, or paintings you would be safe, it would seem likely, if you selected some classic, old or modern, with which you are familiar or of which most critics tend to approve.

What is desirable, however, is for you to develop your own standards of evaluation, to judge for yourself the lasting value of a piece of literature, especially a contemporary work or a lesser known older one, and to be satisfied with your own judgment even though it may not be endorsed by the critic. What is there in a literary work that *gives* it lasting value? Why is something worth reading again and again?

It may be helpful as a start to define literature so that we will know what it is that we are evaluating. In its broadest sense, all written matter is literature—even the pamphlets in an auto salesroom. But these certainly will not endure, nor will catalogs, instructional material, news items, or even most editorials. Let us offer a narrower definition that considers literature as an art form. Let us define *literature* as the artistic recording of personal experiences.* Literature should deal with the experience of an individual as an individual, not as a member of a group. It must deal with individual man, not collective man. And, in dealing with such, the writer must be skilled, the writing itself must be artistic.

This then, is our beginning. We set out to judge the worth of the personal experience depicted and the artistry with which this experience is recorded: that is to say, we are concerned with evaluating the content and the form of the selection.

These two aspects of literature can be compared to the two sides of a coin: one side is the content, or the subject matter written about (the experience); the other side is the form, or the manner in which it is written (the artistry). The literary "coin" itself is cast in words; but when we examine it on the content side, we note the meaning behind the words, and when we examine it on the reverse, we note how the words are put together—the style of the author. And, just as we learn to detect the counterfeit from the genuine coin by a trained recognition of the details of the designs on either side, so we can learn to detect the second-rate (or third-rate) from the first-rate piece of literature by a trained recognition of that which makes for sound content, on the one hand, and for pleasing form on the other.

When we know that the content is sound and the form pleasing we have the assurance that the selection is genuine, that it has lasting value. Then we may or may not wish to study it further, make it our own, and work to interpret it orally to others. But if we do like it, we know that our time will have been well spent.

A literary work cannot be judged solely for content or solely for form. We are just as dissatisfied with a sound idea wretchedly expressed as we are with a puny idea whose form of expression is exemplary. At best the one is a rough diamond, the other tinsel.

It is not necessary that you limit your search to the heaviest and loftiest works of man. The "coin of the realm," which is genuine, has value and is worth keeping regardless of size or denomination. So, a pleasant couplet like Ogden Nash's

* Bacon and Breen conceive of literature as a sort of a trinity of experience in which "the experience of an individual called the *writer* and the experience of another individual called the *reader* . . . are brought together through a third experience called the *work of art,*" Wallace Bacon and Robert Breen, *Literature as Experience,* McGraw-Hill, 1959, p. 12.

The cow is of the bovine ilk;
One end is moo, the other milk.*

is a good coin of a smaller denomination just as a magnificent couplet like Alexander Pope's

True wit is nature to advantage dressed,
What oft was thought, but ne're so well expressed.

is a good coin of a larger denomination. The one is a rollicking shift from classification to "nonsensification"; the other is an apt definition happily and succinctly expressed.

The search for criteria, then, narrows down to a consideration of the lasting value of the content of a literary work and of the form in which it is written. Your final selection, of course, must be guided by your own sense of competency in reading the material aloud. Dialect and characterization, for instance, are relatively easy for some and difficult for others.

The guides that follow will apply to any type or any period of literature—prose or poetry, the tragic or the comic, the classic or the romantic, the well known or the little known, the old or the new. They need not all be applied equally to each work you examine, nor are they mutually exclusive. They certainly are not the only criteria to use. Feel free to use them, to select criteria of various literary critics, or to devise criteria of your own. No one should tell another what he must or must not like, nor even what is or is not "good." One is as free to select a book to read as he is to select a candidate for office—but he should be able to justify his choice, if only to himself. We are suggesting here areas of inquiry rather than objects of inquiry, formulas for finding X rather than values for X, the "how" rather than the "what."

2 GUIDES TO SOUND CONTENT

a Does it have universal appeal?

Literature is concerned with experience, and the more universal the experience the more it will be accepted as true. If the experiences of the soldiers of Troy described in Homer's *Iliad* are the experiences of the twentieth-century soldier; and if the

---

* From *Verses from 1929 On* by Ogden Nash. Copyright 1931 by Ogden Nash. Reprinted by permission of Little, Brown & Co.

experiences of people in Shakespeare's England, Dante's Italy, Don Quixote's Spain, Hans Christian Andersen's Denmark, and Omar Khayyam's Persia are the experiences of people in San Francisco, Kansas City, and New York we have reason to believe that writers such as these will endure. There is a universality of appeal here.

Universality of appeal is no less intense in a work of art because of changing times or differing situations or values, for human experience is constant. We recognize woman's desire for race preservation in Aristophanes' *Lysistrata* just as we do in Stephen Vincent Benét's "Nightmare for Future Reference." Similarly we recognize woman's ambition in Thackeray's Becky Sharp just as we do in Margaret Mitchell's Scarlet O'Hara. Though we may not be bankers we become absorbed in speculating as to whether we would advance or retreat on the road to success if we were confronted with the decision of the protagonist in John P. Marquand's *Point of No Return*. Aren't all of us concerned with a value system that imposes the death penalty on a white man for killing an Arab in Algeria not because of his crime but because of his character? (He failed to express sufficient sorrow in public at his mother's funeral—a situation central to the plot of Albert Camus's *The Stranger*.) What men live for and fight for and die for are the focal points of such works as Stephen Vincent Benét's *John Brown's Body* and Thomas Mann's *Magic Mountain*. However different the circumstances and the value systems of different ages and places may be, there is a constancy in human experience. The plots and themes of love and hate, of success and failure, and of matter and spirit will always have universal appeal if the experiences are real.

Trivial plots and themes, of course, will not have universal appeal. Capsule thinking seldom satisfies. We find tiring essays that glitter with generalities, and the formula story is very dull indeed. Nor do we care for mystery stories that deliberately mislead us by substituting false clues for clever plot.

Look for the universal appeal that lies behind and beyond the particular scene and circumstance of time and place, that reflects mankind's common experiences, and that is constant because human nature is constant.

b   Does it have a richness of association?

It is not enough that the experiences depicted in literature are real and, in consequence, have universal appeal; they must also have an appeal for us, personally. Such an appeal is likely when it is possible for us to associate the experiences presented by the author with our own experiences.

Our experience comes to us through sense perception and we cannot think or read or speak on a level of abstraction very long without running out of "fuel." We need contact with reality, and we depend on our senses to make this contact by supplying us with images of the outside world.

Accordingly, we enjoy literature that employs vivid and satisfying *imagery,* for we can enrich our own experience by associating the images furnished by the author with our own. There are, of course, images other than visual and auditory. There is the tactile (sense of touch), the olfactory (sense of smell), the gustatory (sense of taste), the thermal (sense of heat or cold), and the kinesthetic (sense of pressure). We find that imagery predominates in poetry, especially when the subject matter is romantic and when natural objects are the theme. But we also find satisfying imagery in prose, as, for example, in the beautiful descriptions of Willa Cather, in the vivid yet simple scenes of Ernie Pyle, and in the realistic touches of Ernest Hemingway. The vividness of the imagery contained in a literary selection will make a richness of association possible and so will have an appeal for us.

We also appreciate literature when we can associate the *feelings* depicted with our own feelings. We are concerned with the things that affect us personally, those things that arouse feelings of pleasantness or unpleasantness. Our feelings are aroused when our well being is at stake: our lives, our status, our reputations, our security. We turn to that which enhances our well being and away from that which threatens it, with corresponding emotional reactions. (Here we consider an emotion as a specific *kind* of a feeling: love, hate, indignation, envy, compassion, and the like.)

The situations and the characters of literature are sometimes so realistically portrayed that the emotions touched upon create corresponding emotions in us, merely by association. We do not necessarily need to shed tears at the death of the heroine or at the "foreclosure of the mortgage," but we are genuinely moved when we sense the reality of a particular, personal application of a universal appeal.

Of course we can enjoy literature that does not arouse in us the particular emotion portrayed providing we are sympathetic to it. A girl whose husband or sweetheart was killed in war might appreciate Amy Lowell's "Patterns" for personal reasons. Another reader, without such a background, might appreciate the poem sympathetically. There may be quite a few who would not appreciate the poem at all, who would say that it is sentimental, not true to life. We are our own best judges of feelings and should be able to distinguish between true sentiment and false sentimentality.

We also judge the worth of a book by the accuracy of *character portrayal*. When we associate the characters of the author with the characters of our experience we are satisfied only when we recognize that they are real people, and that they are not masks or stereotypes. The characters in Eugene O'Neill's *The Great God Brown* are masks, as are the characters in *Pilgrim's Progress,* but there are real characters underneath the symbolic ones. You will find true characters in *The Canterbury Tales* and in much of Shakespeare, in John Galsworthy's *Forsyte Saga* and happily enough, in James Thurber. Read his *Family Album* (and even look at his cartoons). But you will not find characters you can associate with real experiences in the formula story, for there the people can be no more real than the plot in which they participate.

You are the judge, of course, as to whether the people in literature are real or not. You must decide whether a character has the substance of real flesh and blood or only of the ink used to describe him.

Read the following story told by Bennett Cerf.* Is the sentiment true? Is the characterization believable? Do you like it?

The heroine of this story was a little eight-year-old girl in a Pennsylvania orphan asylum, so painfully shy and unattractive, and with such annoying mannerisms that she was shunned by the other children and regarded as an insoluble problem by the teachers. Two other asylums had managed to have her transferred, and now, once again, the director and her assistants were seeking only some pretext for getting rid of her themselves.

One afternoon it appeared that an opportunity had arrived. An ironclad rule held that any communication from a child in the institution had to be approved by the director or a

* "Love and Farewell," from "Cerfboard," *This Week,* 25 December 1960. Reprinted by permission of Bennett Cerf.

house mistress before it could be mailed. Now the little girl had been observed stealing down to the main gate and carefully secreting a letter in the branches of a tree that overhung the wall of the asylum. The director and her assistant could scarcely conceal their elation.

They hurried down to the brick wall. Sure enough, the note was visible through the branches of the tree.

The director pounced on it and tore open the envelope. Then she hung her head and passed the note in silence to her assistant. It read: "To anybody who finds this: I love you."

c Does it have individuality of approach?

We search for the universal appeal of a selection and we appreciate the richness of association that makes it particularly appealing to us, but we also want something different. We are intrigued by an author's individuality. Individuality requires *imagination,* the ability to create new ideas and images and to combine and relate old ones to each other in new and unusual ways. When such treatment puts our own imagination to work we are pleased and satisfied.

Any literary work dealing with life after death, for instance, is bound to be unique, but the imagination required to produce *The Divine Comedy* has rarely been equaled. Again, speculation on the shape of things to come challenges the imagination. We have come to appreciate the perspicuity as well as the originality Jules Verne revealed in his novels of the future (which is now the present); and today we read with interest mixed with some trepidation Aldous Huxley's *Brave New World* and George Orwell's *1984.*

A writer does not have to deal with the grandiose and the spectacular, however, to display a keen imaginative sense. Robert Frost's "Stopping by Woods on a Snowy Evening" and Carl Sandburg's "Fog" are highly imaginative; yet they deal with the commonest of subjects, snow and fog. The parables of Jesus are highly imaginative, for they clarify and personalize principles of right conduct; yet they deal with such common subjects as sowing seed, working in a vineyard, and attending a wedding.

Imagination can work best when it is aided by *suggestion* rather than explicit detail. One of the charms of Wordsworth's "The Solitary Reaper" lies in the images and motives he does *not* describe but merely suggests to our imagination. Have you ever read Walter de la Mare's "The Listeners"? Didn't your imagination work overtime on the things that were left unsaid, imagining the

> . . . host of phantom listeners
> That dwelt in the lone house . . .

and how

> . . . the silence surged softly backward,
> When the plunging hoofs were gone.*

You will want to select literature that opens up vistas of things different from what you have previously conceived. You will welcome the individual approach of the author who can set your imagination to work.

The expression of *humor* is also a highly individual matter, for it is the unique way of putting ideas together that do not ordinarily belong together. Humor requires a sense of the incongruous, so the richer one's experiences are and the more developed his sense of values the more he can appreciate the incongruity of a situation or the attempt to poke fun at false values.

Humor is present in its most elemental form in slapstick comedy where pies are thrown in faces of innocent bystanders, snowballs knock the hats off dignified gentlemen, and tacks are placed on chairs of schoolteachers. This is incongruity of situation. In literature, the pun, the limerick, and the "shaggy dog" story are some of the most elementary forms of humor. The pun represents an incongruity of words. The postmaster tells his wife he is "off to the old stamping grounds." The limerick is humorous because of absurd word combinations,

> A lady there was of Antigua
> Who said to her spouse, "What a pig you are!"
> He answered, "My Queen,
> Is it manners you mean,
> Or do you refer to my fig-u-ah?"

* Reprinted by permission of the Literary Trustees of Walter de la Mare and The Society of Authors as their representative.

The "shaggy dog" story is an incongruity of logic, such as the one told of the man with a bleeding ear who explained to the doctor that he had bitten himself. When asked how that was possible, he replied, "Oh, I stood on a chair."

A more sophisticated sense of humor is found in satire. One of the most vitriolic satires is Jonathan Swift's *A Modest Proposal,* offered as a solution to the potato famine in Ireland. He proposed that the famine could be relieved if people ate their babies. The babies would no longer be hungry, for they would be eaten, those eating them would no longer be hungry, obviously, and there would be enough potatoes left for the others. Swift's *Gulliver's Travels* was a less biting but equally potent satire on British politics. Lewis Carroll's *Alice in Wonderland* is gentle satire. We might mention two contemporary satires, Don Marquis's *Archie and Mehitabel* and George Orwell's *Animal Farm.* (It is interesting to note that in all of these satires but the first one mentioned, animals are used to represent people.)

The individual approach is the imaginative approach, whether the intent be serious or humorous. Our appreciation of the individuality of the author will grow as our own imaginative sense develops. We can facilitate this development by reading widely and wisely. We appreciate the new when we are familiar with the old.

3   GUIDES TO PLEASING FORM

Let us now turn the "coin" over and look at the way the words are put together on the printed page; let us consider the artistry of composition.

a   Does it have clarity of organization?

Regardless of the subject matter of a literary work, we want to be able to recognize its *structure* and to follow its development from beginning to end. In an essay or a speech we want to find the specific purpose and to note the sequence of leading ideas with their subdivisions as this purpose is accomplished. If there are digressions we want to recognize them so that we won't lose the train of thought. In a story or a play we expect to follow the development of plot and subplot. We are annoyed if characters appear out of and disappear into nowhere. In poetry (its forms and types will be described in Chapter VI) we expect the poet to develop his thoughts according to the rules of conventional metered verse, and we expect equal satisfaction in following the original structure of free verse. Whether it is conventional or free verse, we tend to reject a poem whose organization is faulty or unclear.

Authors belonging to the "stream-of-consciousness" school, or who employ the associational flashback technique must also achieve clarity of organization. With them we look for psychological rather than logical order. Can you find it in James Joyce's *Ulysses?* You will have less trouble with *The View from Pompey's Head* by Hamilton Basso. In *The War Lovers* by John Hersey, once the alternating pattern of chapter headings becomes clear ("The Raid" measured in hours and "The Tour" measured in days) you are more likely to be satisfied with the originality of the organization.

Whatever else we look for in our selection of good literature we observe that "order is heaven's first law," and seek clarity of organization.

b   Does it have artistry of movement?

We look for an organized structure in a selection but we also look for a satisfying *movement* from thought to thought as that structure is developed. By "movement" we mean the progression in time which is central to oral reading but which is not easily discernible in the configuration of words on the printed page. How are the parts put together? Are there apt transitions, significant repetitions, subtle variations, a pace that is neither too fast nor too slow? We like the identicalness of the refrain found in such classic ballads as "The Twa Sisters" and "Edward," or in the modern ballad, Kipling's "The Ballad of East and West," for example, and we also like the variation in the refrain of "Lord Randal" or in William Rose Benét's "Jesse James" (both of which appear in the text). Notice the lightninglike movement of Ernest Gann's breath-taking adventure story, *The High and the Mighty,* the leisurely pace with which an atmosphere of languor is created in Tennyson's "The Lotos-eaters," the shifts in speed from mood to mood or setting to setting as may be found in Edwin Arlington Robinson's "Tristram" or Somerset Maugham's *Of Human Bondage.*

Artistry of movement is also discernible in a *sequence of sound* in alliteration, in assonance, in rhythm and cadence. We will discuss these in detail in Chapter VI. Here we wish to call to your attention that an artistic sequence of sound in both prose and poetry is a mark of excellence. This, of course, is a prime consideration in reading aloud, for the sounds embedded in the printed page will be revealed for their true worth when produced orally.

The artistry of the author (as well as of the oral reader) must not be too conspicuous or we will be distracted from the content of his work and displeased with his writing. As noted before, "true art conceals art."

SUMMARY

Beginning with a definition of literature as an artistic recording of personal experience, we have devised a set of Guides to the content of the experience and to the artistic form in which it is expressed that will help you in your selection of material that you will enjoy and that you may wish to read aloud.

In regard to content:

Does it have universal appeal, so that the experiences recorded ring true regardless of time, place, point of view, and seriousness of treatment?

Does it have a richness of association that permits us personally to associate the experiences presented by the author with our own experiences, and so appreciate the images that are conjured up, the feelings aroused, and the characters revealed?

Does it have an individual approach in which we are intrigued by the author's individuality and by his imaginative treatment of subject matter, whether it be serious or humorous, and by his ability to set our own imaginations to work?

In regard to form:

Does it have clarity of organization, so that we can recognize the structure and follow the development of thought and mood?

Does it have artistry of movement, so that there is satisfaction in noting the sequence of thoughts and of sounds following each other that will delight our inner ear and the ears of our listeners?

4   STUDIES IN SELECTION

Here are some sample studies in which we give our reasons for selecting material that we enjoy reading to ourselves and to others. As you will notice we don't apply the criteria previously discussed rigorously. They have merely guided us in our choice. Nor have we attempted to apply all of the criteria each time in making our selection. We are struck by the seriousness of a particular theme, we laugh at this passage, or we are deeply stirred by another, or we are intrigued by the individuality of a characterization or with a cluster of unusual images. Similarly we are pleased with the symmetrical structure of a work or even of a passage. We enjoy the smooth flow of thought after thought in a selection, or feel ourselves to be in time with the cadence of a piece of prose or sense the unusual rhythm of a poem.

We hope that you will find the Guides useful in choosing selections of your own.

In the Studies that follow we will refer to a particular point made in the Guides either by italics or by parentheses.

The Old Man and the Sea

BY ERNEST HEMINGWAY

This story reads wonderfully well and it is *worth* reading. With unusual penetration it grasps the elemental conflict between man and nature, and, at the same time, the elemental congruity between man and nature.

The conflict is made poignantly realistic by a succession of detailed images, each one startlingly clear. The response of the fishing line to the action of the marlin (kinesthetic image), the fish as it leaps in the air and as its shadow passes beneath the boat (visual image), the pain in hand and back as the old man endeavors to control the line (tactile image), the savagery and unbelievable ugliness of the sharks' attack (visual, auditory, and kinesthetic images), the taste of blood and sweat (gustatory image), the final prostration of the old man on the newspapers on his cot (tactile and thermal images) exemplify but a few.

The attempt to bridge the gap between man and nature reminds us of Kenneth Burke's * explanation of mystery.

> Mystery arises at that point where different *kinds* of beings are in communication. In mystery there must be *strangeness,* but the estranged must be thought of as in some way capable of communion. There is mystery in an animal's eyes at those

* *A Rhetoric of Motive,* New York, 1950, p. 115.

moments when a man feels that he and the animal understand each other in some inexpressible fashion.

Not only has Hemingway succeeded in expressing the "inexpressible" understanding between the old man and the fish; he
has also revealed the mystery of communion between the old
man and the water itself—beings utterly different in kind. (Use of
imagination)

We admire, naturally, the indomitable will of the protagonist,
and we admire the faith of the boy in this ancient man. And
somehow we are made to realize that fullness and richness of life
are completely attainable despite poverty and physical failure.
(Universality of appeal)

The form adjusts to the content especially in *sound sequences.*
The words are short, an extraordinary preponderance of monosyllables; the sentences are simple and relatively equal in length.
Thus, a cadence results that is hypnotic; the attention centers on
the primitive essence of the narrative, undistracted by any break
in continuity. In consequence there is an unbelievable speed of
movement. The story is quickly over, but it makes a lasting impression.

The Red Pony

BY JOHN STEINBECK

The Old Man and the Sea is basically an allegory, for the characters are symbols of humanity. The reader recognizes its truth
as he becomes aware of the attributes shared by all alike. (Universality of appeal) The characters in *The Red Pony,* however,
are individual and startlingly real. If the reader does not already
recognize them in himself or in people about him, he will soon
come to know them intimately. (Richness of association)

It is the story of a boy, Jody Tiflin, living with his family on a
west coast ranch, who finally gets what he has longed for most
of his young life—a red pony colt. The animal falls sick and
Jody sleeps in the barn with it. When it dies, Jody madly fights
the buzzards flying low for "the moment of death they know so
well." That is the story, but the details of characterization raise
it to such heights that it can be read and reread by young and old.

The blind obedience and trust, poignantly unjustified, of Jody;

the way he builds up the worth of his possession to his schoolmates, trivial to the adult but enormously important to the child; the sympathy of the hired man, Billy Buck, whose low social status and lack of technical skill hasten the tragedy; the thick-skinned father in whom kindness and justice are poorly proportioned; the intimacy that is shared between Jody and his mother that fails utterly to help him in his hour of need—all of these details of *characterization* recall experiences we have lived or fancied or witnessed and which penetrate deep and remain. (Arouses feeling)

The *sequence of thought* moves at a satisfying speed. The action does not move ahead of the characterization. Neither is the reader tempted to skip the characterization to discover the direction of the unfolding plot. We share the excitement of impending tragedy but we choose to share it at a speed paced by the train of thought in Jody's mind. Then when disillusionment, despair, resolve, and action come, we are ready, for they come to him and to us simultaneously.

How Love Came to General Grant *

BY DONALD OGDEN STEWART
IN THE MANNER OF HAROLD BELL WRIGHT

It's fun to read *How Love Came to General Grant* providing you are familiar with the personal habits of the general and know something of the nature of Harold Bell Wright; for the *humor* lies both in the discrepancy between his actual behavior and that related in the story and in the manner of telling the story. We laugh at the description of the general as a fine elegantly attired gentleman whose life is free from dissipation of any sort and whose conversation is brilliant and free from any taint of coarseness. We are likewise amused at the sticky bits of Victorian sentimentality that permeate the story. Getting into the spirit of the thing we will enjoy the scene in which dear little unclad Ella, "slowly sinking for the third time" rather than scream for help, was horrified to discover that a bearded stranger was swimming rapidly toward her—"but her shame was soon changed to joy when she realized that he was purposely keeping his eyes tight shut."

* Maud May Babcock, *Interpretative Selections for Colleges,* The University Publishing Co., New York, 1930, pp. 279-86.

There is humor in the form of the story, too, both in *sound sequence* and in *structure*. "The palatial Fifth Avenue place of Cornelius van der Griff was brilliantly lighted with many brilliant lights" is a playful redundancy. The appendages "Nor were they far from wrong" to a particularly gushy paragraph of sentiment, and "Need I name her" to a paragraph chock full of a virtuous account of the unnamed girl give added humor. The abrupt changes in pace at the end of pious platitudes provide apt transitions between reflection and narration. The balancing of a short simple statement with a lengthier sentiment as in the last lines of the story

"General," she began.

"Miss Flowers," said the strong man, simply, "Call me Ulysses."

is typical of the sentence structure throughout.

The Story Teller

BY H. H. MUNRO (SAKI)

There is the humor of manners in *How Love Came to General Grant*. There is humor of another sort in *The Story Teller* by Saki —the humor of relief. Most realistically, Saki depicts the failure of a maidenly aunt to subdue a small boy and two small girls in a railway carriage. The insatiable "Why?" of a child is an experience that rings true to life for everyone. (Universality of appeal) When the bachelor satiates the children by telling the story of a girl who was "horribly good" we join the aunt in a gasp of admiration. That the story is "highly improper" adds to rather than lessens our enjoyment. It was not told to *our* children.

The imagery is choice. The *visual* images of the dull countryside of the main story and the exciting aspects of the prince's garden in the bachelor's story; the *auditory* image of the clinking of "metal medals" and of the song, "The Road to Mandalay"; and the *tactile* image of an uncomfortable compartment seat afford the principal means of introducing humor and excitement.

There is real artistry in the development of the stories within a story. The sudden shifts to attention from inattention and the recurrence of the eternal "Why?" all contribute to the delight of this satisfying yarn. (Organization and movement)

Parting

BY EMILY DICKINSON

My life closed twice before its close;
    It yet remains to see
If Immortality unveil
    A third event to me,

So huge, so hopeless to conceive,
    As these that twice befell.
Parting is all we know of heaven,
    And all we need of hell.

There is an almost mystical beauty in this short poem. There
are no distracting thoughts. There are no discordant notes. Few
experiences are more universal in their appeal.

It takes imagination to equate "parting" with both "heaven"
and "hell" in the last two verses. Repetition can render it only
more beautiful. There is deep penetration, indeed, when one is
brought face to face with both life and death in two short stanzas.
(Arouses feeling)

The form leaves nothing to be desired. The regular simple alternation of iambic tetrameter and iambic trimeter with an *a b c b*
rhyme scheme lends itself to a slow, stately, sad, rhythmic movement. (Artistry of movement) There is just one irregular line,
the third verse in the second stanza. The substitution of a trochee
"parting" for an iamb brings out that title word in bold relief. The
thought of "heaven" accentuates the finality, the irrevocability of
the last word of the poem, "hell." (The metrical terms used here
are explained in Chapter VI.)

Loveliest of Trees

BY A. E. HOUSMAN *

Loveliest of trees, the cherry now
Is hung with bloom along the bough,

* From *Complete Poems* by A. E. Housman. Copyright 1924, c 1959,
by Holt, Rinehart & Winston, Inc. Reprinted by permission of the publish-

And stands about the woodland ride
Wearing white for Eastertide.

Now, of my threescore years and ten,
Twenty will not come again,
And take from seventy springs a score,
It only leaves me fifty more.

And since to look at things in bloom
Fifty springs are little room,
About the woodlands I will go
To see the cherry hung with snow.

A Shropshire Lad, the volume in which this poem appears, is pure song from cover to cover. The images appear sharp before the senses, and the thoughts relating to them tap many of our innermost experiences. (Richness of association) Perhaps some are vicarious, such as those associated with infidelity and death. But "Loveliest of Trees" is very much alive, and the experience is very real.

The appreciation of the lyric consists as much in what it does not say as in what it does say. The dividing line between true sentiment and false sentimentality is never crossed. (The feelings aroused) The bloom of the cherry bough is deserving of an Eastertide setting. And that is all. This is the major image and it is the focus of attention. There is a pleasantly humorous arithmetic calculation, but it is not nostalgic. Then there is the sensible decision to take a walk and look at the trees. When no false note is rung, the beauty of the true note is enhanced. One can appreciate this lovely scene without embarrassment.

The rhythmic scheme is simple, iambic tetrameter with an *a a b b* rhyme. The tendency to a sing-song jingle is skillfully suppressed by the frequent substitution of trochaic feet. (Artistry of movement)

"Loveliest of Trees," called by some the most beautiful lyric in the English language, is the quintessence of simplicity.

ers, and of The Society of Authors as literary representatives of the Estate of the late A. E. Housman and Messrs. Jonathan Cape, Ltd., publishers of A. E. Housman's *Collected Poems.*

Nightmare Number Three *

BY STEPHEN VINCENT BENÉT

(The revolt of the machine is the subject matter.)

We had expected everything but revolt
And I kind of wonder myself when they started thinking—
But there's no dice to that now.
. . . I guess they got tired of us
And the whole smell of human hands . . .

There is a note of horror underlying this poem, for the possibility of realization of the world it presents is uncomfortably close. The *imagination* is stirred by the unusual personification of the machines and by the boldness of the *imagery* employed. Familiar as we are with the machine age of which we are so much a part, we are forced by the poem to recognize the distortion of values traceable in so many instances to the overdependence of man on the machine for his well-being, not to mention his very existence. We are faced with the proposition: spiritual values should be restored, even at the expense of material values. (Universality of appeal)

It is not so much the reversal of power from man to the machine that causes the "nightmare" to linger in our consciousness so long after we experience it through the reading; it is our acknowledgment of the diabolical justice of the actions of the machines who now possess our sensitivity and our morality.

And I'd go down in a minute and take my chance—
I'm a good American and I've always liked them—
Except for one small detail that bothers me
And that's the food proposition. Because you see,
The concrete-mixer may have made a mistake,
And it looks like just high spirits,
But, if it's got so they like the flavor—well—

* From *Selected Works of Stephen Vincent Benét,* Holt, Rinehart, & Winston, Inc. Copyright 1933, 1935, 1938 by Stephen Vincent Benét. Reprinted by permission of Brandt and Brandt.

Written in free verse, *Nightmare Number Three* possesses a rhythmic pattern, metallic and impersonal. This impersonal feeling—the doctrine of dialectical materialism expresses it—is intensified by the careless, matter of fact, conversational "patter" of the narrator. There are no pyrotechnics here. The disarming casualness with which the separate thoughts are woven together (Artistry of movement) seems only to intensify the horror of what has happened and what is about to happen.

If you enjoy this poem you will also enjoy the other Nightmares: *Nightmare for Future Reference* and *Metropolitan Nightmare.**

The Gettysburg Address †

Each of us has read and reread the Gettysburg Address. There can be no doubt that it was a magnificent speech. One need only apply the canons of rhetoric to ascertain this. But it is also great literature, for it can be appreciated in terms other than its effect upon an audience.

We are appreciative of its simplicity and its brevity. We are impressed by the earnestness and the sincerity of Lincoln the man, by his unique conception of the dedication of a battlefield through the continuing good deeds of the living. (Universality of appeal)

The most striking feature of all, however, might well be the extraordinary *imaginative* concept set forth in the opening and repeated in the closing lines.

. . . our fathers brought forth upon this continent a new nation conceived in liberty and dedicated to the proposition that all men are created equal . . . we here highly resolve . . . that the nation under God shall have a new birth of freedom . . .

It is the beautiful and startlingly original concept whereby natural birth is equated to the birth of a nation that so stirs our imagination. The thought is so basic, so universal, so exciting, so completely appealing. This concept alone, the mystical birth of America, is reason enough for the lasting value of the address.

The content is memorable, but so also is the form. Here is prose

* These poems appear in their entirety in Chapter VII, pp. 187-97.
† See text, page 79.

barely distinguishable from poetry, the rhythm is so marked. Specifically, the rhythmic cadence is the product of both the *beauty of the sentence structure* and the *artistry of movement*. A well-nigh perfect balance is achieved through intriguing repetitions and overlappings. Let us illustrate.

In the second sentence "that nation or any nation so conceived and so dedicated" repeats the phrasing of the first sentence. Similarly, in the third sentence, "We are met on a great battlefield of that war" repeats the phrasing of the second. In the fourth, the opening words are identical with the third. "We are met . . ." And so on.

In the second paragraph Lincoln chose one adjective to modify devotion—"increased devotion"—in designating the role of the living. See how he equates this to the augmented modification of the word in "their last full measure of devotion," which designates the role of the dead. Notice, too, the skillful variation in the structure of the two successive lines: "It is for us the living, rather to be dedicated . . ." and "It is rather for us to be here dedicated . . ." And, finally, listen to the stately cadence of "the government of the people, by the people, and for the people . . ."

IV

ASSIMILATION OF MATERIAL

> Some books are to be tasted, others to be swallowed,
> and some few to be chewed or digested—that is,
> some books are to be read only in parts, others to
> be read, but not curiously, and some few to be read
> wholly, and with diligence and attention.
>
> FRANCIS BACON

In your search for good literature to read aloud you will skim over some selections, read others through, and that's the end of it; but when you have found something you believe to be worth while, you owe it to yourself and certainly to those who are going to listen to you read, to "chew and digest" it. *You must assimilate what you read.*

The "chewing" is the more difficult part, but it is vitally necessary. This is the job of *comprehending the material.* Comprehension involves analysis: analysis of meaning, analysis of structure (syntax and thought development), and analysis of the purpose, mood, and times of the author. The "digesting" is the easier but no less important part. It consists of *reflecting upon the material* so as to form a synthesis: permitting the connotation of words to enter your consciousness, associating the experiences, and drawing upon your imagination to fill in the gaps.*

Assimilation is a logical step in your preparation for reading aloud between selection and presentation. In fact it is imperative that you become thoroughly familiar with the material you have so carefully selected before you attempt to interpret it successfully to others. A glib oral reader having acquired facility only in utilizing vocal techniques may transmit words themselves pleasantly enough but seldom the meaning behind the words and seldom in a manner best suited to convey the meaning.

* As you study this chapter, notice how the topics treated relate to the Guides to selection of material discussed in Chapter III.

1 COMPREHENSION

a Comprehending the meaning

In the first place we certainly want to know the exact meaning of single words, what the words denote. There are many and sometimes even common English words in a selection which will prevent or obscure our understanding of the whole unless we look them up. Of importance, too, are the meanings of the allusions, references, and figures of speech. Suppose you are going to read the well-known sonnet by Keats, "On First Looking into Chapman's Homer."

> Much have I travell'd in the realms of gold,
> And many goodly states and Kingdoms seen;
> Round many western islands have I been
> Which bards in fealty to Apollo hold.
> Oft of one wide expanse have I been told
> That deep-browed Homer ruled as his demesne;
> Yet did I never breathe its pure serene
> Till I heard Chapman speak out loud and bold:
> Then felt I like some watcher of the skies
> When a new planet swims into his ken;
> Or like stout Cortez when with eagle eyes
> He star'd at the Pacific—and all his men
> Look'd at each other with a wild surmise—
> Silent upon a peak in Darien.

Unless you knew that "bard" means "poet," "fealty" means "loyalty," "demesne" means "domain," and "ken" means "consciousness," your reading would convey little if any meaning to your listeners. Not only would the emphasis be faulty but you would be lacking in the "full realization of the content of your words as you utter them" and you certainly would not have that "lively sense of communication."

Then, in addition to the words, there are the references, the allusions, and at least one figure of speech that must be comprehended in this sonnet. Why do bards, for instance, hold the western islands in fealty to Apollo? The chances are that most people have heard of Homer, but have they heard of Chapman, or need they? Where is Darien? And wasn't it Balboa rather than Cortez who discovered the Pacific Ocean? What sort of feeling is engendered by the figure "a new planet swims into his ken"? These questions must all be answered; or some parts of the poem will remain fuzzy.

b Comprehending the structure

A familiarity with the structure of your selection is likewise indispensable to an adequate preparation. There is the structure within the sentence, or the syntax, to consider and likewise the structure of the entire selection, the thought development. Without a clear understanding of the syntax you will garble the sentence. Without a clear picture of thought development you may distort or destroy the symmetry of the entire selection. Let us first exemplify the importance of understanding syntax.

This chapter begins with a quotation from Bacon's essay "Of Studies." Wayland Maxfield Parrish in *Reading Aloud* quotes another passage from the same essay to illustrate the problem of grasping meaning. Parrish quotes without punctuation marks; but even *with* them, comprehension is provokingly difficult.

Histories make men wise, poets witty, the mathematics subtle, natural philosophy deep, moral grave, logic and rhetoric able to contend.

On first reading it would appear that histories make men all these things, yet how can histories make men witty or make the mathematics subtle? Then, what kind of a grave is a "moral grave"? When we finally discover that this is a compound sentence containing a series of ellipses, and that "moral" modifies "philosophy," the meaning is no longer obscure (assuming you know the definitions of natural and of moral philosophy). Now try expanding the sentence to be sure you get it. "Histories make men wise, poets make men witty, the mathematics make men subtle, natural philosophy (science) makes men deep, moral philosophy (theology) makes men grave, logic and rhetoric (the art of persuasion) make men able to contend." This is a somewhat lengthy analysis, but one missing link will destroy the entire chain.

Consider the beautiful sonnet by Wordsworth "Composed Upon Westminster Bridge."

Earth has not anything to show more fair:
Dull would he be of soul who could pass by
A sight so touching in its majesty:
This City now doth like a garment wear
The beauty of the morning; silent, bare,
Ships, towers, domes, theatres, and temples lie
Open unto the fields, and to the sky;
All bright and glittering in the smokeless air.
Never did sun more beautifully steep
In his first splendour valley, rock, or hill;
Ne'er saw I, never felt, a calm so deep!
The river glideth at his own sweet will:
Dear God! the very houses seem asleep
And all that mighty heart is lying still!

So much can be said about this sonnet * that it is difficult to confine ourselves to the problems of syntax alone, but appreciation will be stillborn unless they are resolved.

The first problem lies in lines 4 and 5. Notice that "City" is the subject, and "doth wear" is the verb, "the beauty of the morning" is the object, and "like a garment" modifies the verb. Once this is clear it becomes evident that "garment" and "wear" cannot be run together and that line 4 is a run-on line. Until this is clear, all we will get out of the lines will be a jingle.

The second problem begins in the last two words of line 5 and carries down to the end of line 8. These two words are adjectives which modify the next five words which are all nouns! These nouns are the subject, "lie open" is the verb, then follow two adverbial modifiers, and finally there is an adjectival phrase, line 8, which modifies the subject.

This may seem like a dull junior high school exercise in sentence diagramming, but there is no other way to comprehend the meaning. Once this syntactical knot is unraveled, the meaning is

* See the study by Mark Van Doren in *An Introduction to Poetry*, William Sloane, New York, 1951, pp. 55-8.

clear, and all of the vocal factors of voice (studied in Chapter II) involved in oral communication can be utilized successfully.

There is one more syntactical problem found in the next two lines, 9 and 10. Can you find it? What is the subject, the verb, the object? To run "beautifully" and "steep" together, and to pause after "steep" can only make gibberish. Why?

The study of thought development is as rewarding as it is instructive. It is essentially a study of symmetry. It has to do with the relationship of parts to each other and to the whole. It is concerned, in a story, with the unfolding of plot and mood and character. It notes acceleration and retardation, uniformity and variation, continuity and digression. When you become thoroughly aware of the manner in which the author develops his thought and perceive how all the parts fit in place you will be able to appreciate the symmetrical beauty of the passage.

Thought development is often determined by the literary form of the selection. In prose you are aided in tracing the development through the paragraphing and the other sectional divisions. A knowledge of the structure of a narrative will guide you in comprehending the thought development of a short story, a novel, or a play. An outline analysis of the leading ideas and their subdivisions will enable you to grasp the structure of non-narrative prose: an essay, a speech, a biographical or historical sketch, or a delightful piece of exposition or description. In poetry, some forms are most rigid, while others, especially those of free verse, are elusive. Since some special knowledge of prosody is necessary for reading poetry intelligently, it will be best to include our study of verse forms in Chapter VI.

All literature is structured, one way or another, to reveal the developing thoughts. You must not neglect a careful analysis of structure either of the part (syntax) or of the whole if you yourself are to understand and if you are to communicate effectively.

c   Comprehending the author

Finally an analysis of the author, his purpose, and his times is helpful but not crucial to the comprehension of the selection you have chosen to study. Bacon and Breen * make the point that we are concerned with the literature rather than the author. A poem, for instance, is an experience, not a document. To know in ad-

* Op. cit., pp. 157-64.

vance, however, what sort of an experience we might anticipate will make us more receptive.

To learn, for instance, that the Cavalier poets were concerned with manners, that they delighted in conceits, and believed nature was never to be experienced in the raw; and that the Romanticists were concerned with deep emotions and with the wonders of nature will enable us to know why Herrick's "Julia" and his "To Daffodils" are so different from Wordsworth's "Lucy" and his "Daffodils," but it will not help us like the one better than the other. If we find pleasure in Shakespeare's sonnet, "When In Disgrace with Fortune and Men's Eyes," the knowledge that the sentiments were addressed to a man instead of a lady might disturb us were it not for the additional knowledge that such sentiments were perfectly proper when addressed to one's patron (as this was). It is interesting but not vital to know which war is referred to in Amy Lowell's "Patterns," A. E. Housman's *A Shropshire Lad,* or Stephen Vincent Benét's "Nightmare for Future Reference."

So, do not miss the opportunity to learn about the author and his times, for it will help you to understand his work; but do not confuse knowledge *about* the work with knowledge *of* the work.

We do not wish to be pedantic in our emphasis on the need for a thorough analysis of the material you have selected to read. Literature is to be enjoyed, not suffered, but you cannot enjoy what you do not comprehend.

2   REFLECTION

Comprehension is a labor of the mind but reflection is a labor of love. We may comprehend, yet remain cold and indifferent; but when we associate the subject matter with our experiences, real or vicarious, or discover that the style of expression harmonizes with our own sense of form or rhythm, or when we are incited to give free rein to our imagination by what we read, then we come to appreciate the material. Reflection may not require the exacting discipline that is needed for thorough comprehension but it does require concentration.

We need time to reflect if we are going to let the connotations of words sink in. Connotation is the suggested rather than the explicit meaning. Take the rare case when the denotation is purposely cut off—Lewis Carroll's "The Jabberwocky" from *Alice in Wonderland:*

> 'Twas brillig, and the slithey toves
> Did gyre and gimble in the wabe;
> All mimsy were the borogoves,
> And the mome raths outgrabe . . .
>
> And as in uffish thought he stood,
> The Jabberwock with eyes of flame,
> Came whiffling through the tulgey wood,
> And burbled as it came!

Since the words mean almost anything within the syntactic structure, you are free to let your imagination run wild and associate what you please with what you think the words mean. There is nothing here *but* connotation.

In Don Marquis's "Tragedy of the Deep," * we encounter these lines:

> There was once an octopus
> Who was very proud of his eight legs . . .
> They were long, and slithery and beautiful.

We are not particularly concerned with the exact meaning of the word "slithery" but we are fascinated by its connotation. We may also take delight in the humor of the juxtaposition of "slithery" and "beautiful." It is analogous to the description of the little girl in Saki's *The Story Teller* who was "horribly good."

Appreciation oftentimes grows slowly within us. When we first read the line from Emily Dickinson "when everything that ticks has stopped," written to describe absolute silence, we think of clocks, all kinds of clocks whose ticks we remember. But, then when reflection sets in, we may envisage all the things we know that have regular sound or even motion: machinery, tides, the

---

* From *Noah an' Jonah an' Cap'n John Smith* by Don Marquis. Copyright 1921, D. Appleton and Company. Reprinted by permission of the publishers Appleton-Century-Crofts, Inc.

sound of katydids, heartbeats. Read Coleridge's *The Rime of the Ancient Mariner.* You may or may not appreciate its moral flavor, the plot development, or the metrical form, but when, upon reflection, you add your own experiences of, for instance, stagnant water, slimy creatures, extreme thirst, heat, etc., you are more than likely to appreciate such lines as:

> The very deep did rot: O Christ!
> That ever this should be!
> Yea, slimy things did crawl with legs
> Upon a slimy sea!

and

> With throats unslaked, with black lips baked,
> We could nor laugh nor wail;
> Through utter drought all dumb we stood!
> I bit my arm, I sucked the blood,
> And cried, "A sail! A sail!"

The more experiences we have, the more background we have, the more imagination we have, the more opportunity there is to appreciate a piece of literature. There is an enchanting chapter in A. G. McDonnell's *England Their England* * that describes the "ancient city of Winchester, city of Alfred, once capital of England, perhaps even the Camelot of Arthur." The descriptions are beautiful, and upon first reading one's imagination will run riot even as did Donald's (the protagonist) when he climbed the slopes of St. Catherine's Hill and "found a little grassy slope which fitted his back like a deck chair at full stretch, and lay down and tilted his hat over his forehead and joined his hands behind his head." As we read we see the High Street, the castle at the top, where Arthur's table is hung, the enormous statue of King Alfred at the bottom, Winchester College beyond that, older even than Harrow and Eton (whose extraordinary motto, "Manners Makyth Man," puts "kindliness above learning"), the water-meads of the river Itchen, the circular trench dug by the Britons as a defense against the Legions; and we hear the sounds of cricket bats, the megaphones of the coaches of the racing-fours, and the bells of

* Macmillan & Co. Ltd., London, 1957.

the Cathedral "deep and far, like the strong clang of Thor's anvil in Valhalla"; and we appreciate all these things because of the many associations we make with all the delightful images.

But now if we summon up our background in English history and English literature (and German mythology) we can begin to reincarnate the days of old, and more images will flow pleasantly into our consciousness, and our appreciation grows. If perchance we have visited Winchester in person, we can add still more. We see the Round Table looking for all the world like a round backgammon board, we notice the majestic imperturbability of King Alfred's statue with a parking lot at its base, we catch sight of gowned school boys sprinting across the inner quad of Winchester College, we view the Itchen and immediately we are positive that here the Lady of Shalott drifted past in her boat, we climb St. Catherine's Hill beyond the still intact Roman walls, and we sit where Donald sat, hear the sounds he heard, and finally before we know it, we gaze with him across the downs and moors a hundred miles away to the lonely, cold, gray shores of Cornwall where Arthur fought his "last great battle of the west," and we are content. This is the reward of reflection.

Six thousand miles from Winchester lies the city of San Francisco. The following vignette of the city viewed from the "Top o' the Mark" by Herb Caen might lose some of its charm if one has not actually spent an hour in this skyroom on top of the Mark Hopkins Hotel, a multi-storied hotel built on top of Nob Hill overlooking the city, the bridges, the distant foothills, the Golden Gate, and the ocean. But if you turn your imagination free and reflect for awhile, you should soon be able to visualize and appreciate the quiet waters of the bay (usually so dark and choppy) and the thousands of white and pink and gray crackerbox houses edged with skyscrapers immediately below. Let the picture become sharp gradually. Let the reflective process continue until to you, too, the drink would seem "awfully flat."

San Francisco, viewed under glass from Top o' the Mark one September night at 7:10, was at its spectacular best—so overwhelmingly beautiful that a hush fell over the crowded room and people crowded silently against the windows to drink in the glamorama . . . Exactly 7:10—and out in the Pacific, the fiery sun slipped with incredible swiftness behind a filmy curtain of far-off clouds—and out of the East Bay hills rose a white full

moon, pale and wonderful . . . Not a ripple broke the ageless
face of the Bay, and across its surface rode a tug pulling a barge,
leaving a wake so long and straight that it seemed to be etched
forever in a stone . . . Behind the Ferry Building dressed up
in its holiday lights of red, white, and blue, rose a smoky plume
from an idling ferryboat—and not a zephyr disturbed the still air
to blow it away . . . As the golden day died slowly before your
eyes, the lights came on in rhythmic twinkles that turned every
street into a river of stop-and-glow lights: a white flood washed
up over Coit Tower—and Telegraph Hill all at once loomed dark
and lumpy, as though somebody had stood back and pelted it
with houses . . . Then the moon was full up, throwing a million
gallons of cream over the black waters under the Bay Bridge . . .
It was now 7:15—five minutes had stretched into infinity—and
slowly the people who had seen almost more than their eyes could
bear walked away from the windows and back to their seats. All
of a sudden, a drink seemed awfully flat.*

Just how does reflection affect interpretation? Provided we
have a thorough comprehension of the meaning and structure of
the selection, reflection will give it a meaning *for us* and will permit the widest, the most sensitive, and the most accurate expression of feeling. In studying the basic techniques of the communi-
cative process we noticed that feeling is revealed principally
through quality of voice, pitch range, intensity, and tempo. Now
we can employ these vocal factors purposefully, for we know
that our interpretation will be true. We will study this process
in the next two chapters.

Assimilation may often be a slow process. We need time before
we comprehend what we read; and we may want time for reflection in order to appreciate it to the full. It should be evident,
however, that time must be taken if we are to read aloud effectively. It may very well be, then, that reading literature aloud,
or, at least, the preparation for reading literature aloud, is the
best and the most satisfying way to enjoy literature.

* From *Don't Call It Frisco* by Herb Caen. Copyright 1953 by Herb
Caen. Reprinted by permission of Doubleday & Company, Inc.

3 A STUDY IN ASSIMILATION

Gift from the Sea

BY ANNE MORROW LINDBERGH

The setting of this book is the sea shore, a very quiet sector of the beach, where Anne Morrow Lindbergh went in search of a "pattern of living" and for a "contemplative corner" where she could learn to adjust to her individual needs as well as to the needs of others.

The book is organized in a series of short chapters, each of which consists of a contemplation touched off by what the author discovers on the beach. The first contemplation provides an awareness of the capacity to relax on the warm soft sand. Then the author contemplates, one by one, various seashells, her gifts from the sea. They give her partial answers to some of life's problems, including a philosophy of marriage.

The first shell, Channelled Whelk, had "housed a whelk, a snail-like creature, and then, temporarily, after the death of the first occupant, a little hermit crab, who had run away, leaving his tracks behind him like a delicate vine on the sand." The shell, so simple, bare, yet beautiful, taught her the meaning and value of simplicity, the antithesis to the complexity of modern daily living.

Then, there was Moon Shell, a snail shell, with its smooth symmetrical face on which is "pencilled with precision a perfect spiral, winding to the pinpoint center . . . the tiny dark core of the apex, the pupil of the eye." The eye stared at her and she stared back. She imagined it to be an "island set in ever widening circles of waves, alone, self-contained, serene." Alone on this "island" she discovered the meaning of solitude.

The next shell, Double-Sunrise, was a delicate bivalve shell, both halves matching exactly, which reminded her of all pure relationships. "The first part of every relationship is pure whether it be with friend or lover, husband or child . . . And then how swiftly . . . the relationship changes; it becomes complicated, encumbered by its contact with the world." The marriage relationship is the one that changes the most, yet it is possible for

the marriage partners to return to the pure relationship of the
sunrise shell briefly, at different times and in different ways.

The Oyster Bed is the shell that expresses the middle years of
marriage. It is humped and uneven and irregular, but it is strong
and binding. In fact there are many bonds in marriage that make
up a web "that is taut and firm. The web is fashioned of love."
If by any chance the romantic love of the double-sunrise shell is
snapped, the many bonds remaining will endure.

Following are two chapters—the first and sixth—from *Gift
from the Sea.**

The Beach

The beach is not the place to work; to read, write or think. I
should have remembered that from other years. Too warm, too
damp, too soft for any real mental discipline or sharp flights of
spirit. One never learns. Hopefully, one carries down the faded
straw bag, lumpy with books, clean paper, long over-due unan-
swered letters, freshly sharpened pencils, lists, and good intentions.
The books remain unread, the pencils break their points, and the
pads rest smooth and unblemished as the cloudless sky. No reading, no writing, no thoughts even—at least, not at first.

At first, the tired body takes over completely. As on shipboard,
one descends into a deck-chair apathy. One is forced against one's
mind, against all tidy resolutions, back into the primeval rhythms
of the sea-shore. Rollers on the beach, wind in the pines, the slow
flapping of herons across sand dunes, drown out the hectic rhythms
of city and suburb, time tables and schedules. One falls under their
spell, relaxes, stretches out prone. One becomes, in fact, like the
element on which one lies, flattened by the sea; bare, open, empty
as the beach, erased by today's tides of all yesterday's scribblings.

And then, some morning in the second week, the mind wakes,
comes to life again. Not in a city sense—no—but beach-wise. It
begins to drift, to play, to turn over in gentle careless rolls like
those lazy waves on the beach. One never knows what chance
treasures these easy unconscious rollers may toss up, on the

* Reprinted by permission of Pantheon Books, Inc.

smooth white sand of the conscious mind; what perfectly rounded stone, what rare shell from the ocean floor. Perhaps a channelled whelk, a moon shell, or even an argonaut.

But it must not be sought for or—heaven forbid!—dug for. No, no dredging of the sea-bottom here. That would defeat one's purpose. The sea does not reward those who are too anxious, too greedy, or too impatient. To dig for treasures shows not only impatience and greed, but lack of faith. Patience, patience, patience, is what the sea teaches. Patience and faith. One should lie empty, open, choiceless as a beach—waiting for a gift from the sea.

Argonauta

There are in the beach-world certain rare creatures, the "Argonauta" (Paper Nautilus), who are not fastened to their shell at all. It is actually a cradle for the young, held in the arms of the mother argonaut who floats with it to the surface, where the eggs hatch and the young swim away. Then the mother argonaut leaves her shell and starts another life. I am fascinated by this image of the argonaut, whose temporary dwelling I have seen only as the treasure of a specialist's collection. Almost transparent, delicately fluted like a Greek column, this narcissus-white snail shell is feather light as some coracle of ancient times, ready to set sail across unknown seas. It was named, the book tells me, for the fabled ships of Jason that went in search of the Golden Fleece. Sailors consider these shells a sign of fair weather and favorable winds.

Lovely shell, lovely image—I am tempted to play with it in my mind. Is this the symbol for another stage in relationships? Can we middle-aged argonauts when we outgrow the oyster bed, look forward to the freedom of the nautilus who has left its shell for the open seas? But what does the open sea hold for us? We cannot believe that the second half of life promises "fair weather and favorable winds." What golden fleece is there for the middle-aged? . . .

Is the golden fleece that awaits us some kind of new freedom for growth? And in this new freedom, is there any place for a relationship? I believe there is, after the oyster bed, an opportunity for the best relationship of all: not a limited, mutually exclusive one, like the sunrise shell; and not a functional, dependent one, as in the oyster bed; but the meeting of two whole fully developed people as persons . . .

But this new relationship of persons as persons, this more human love, this two solitudes conception is not something that comes easily. It must have grown, like all firm-rooted growth, slowly. It perhaps can only follow a long development in the history of human civilization and individually in each human being's life. Such a stage in life, it would seem to me, must come not as a gift or a lucky accident, but as part of an evolutionary process, an achievement which could only follow certain important developments in each partner. . . .

A good relationship has a pattern like a dance and is built on some of the same rules. The partners do not need to hold on tightly, because they move confidently in the same pattern, intricate but gay and swift and free, like a country dance of Mozart's. To touch heavily would be to arrest the pattern and freeze the movement, to check the endlessly changing beauty of its unfolding. There is no place here for the possessive clutch, the clinging arm, the heavy hand: only the barest touch in passing. Now arm in arm, now face to face, now back to back—it does not matter which. Because they know they are partners moving to the same rhythm, creating a pattern together, and being invisibly nourished by it.

The joy of such a pattern is not only the joy of creation or the joy of participation, it is also the joy of living in the moment. Lightness of touch and living in the moment are intertwined. One cannot dance well unless one is completely in time with the music, not leaning back to the last step or pressing forward to the next one, but poised directly on the present step as it comes. Perfect poise on the beat is what gives good dancing its sense of ease, of timelessness, of the eternal. It is what Blake was speaking of when he wrote:

He who bends to himself a joy
Doth the winged life destroy;
But he who kisses the joy as it flies
Lives in Eternity's sunrise.

The dancers who are perfectly in time never destroy "the winged life" in each other or in themselves.

But how does one learn this technique of the dance? Why is it so difficult? What makes us hesitate and stumble? It is fear, I think, that makes one cling nostalgically to the last moment or clutch greedily toward the next. Fear destroys "the winged life." But how to exorcise it? It can only be exorcised by its opposite, love. When the heart is flooded with love there is no room in it for fear, for doubt, for hesitation. And it is this lack of fear that makes for the dance. When each partner loves so completely that he has forgotten to ask himself whether or not he is loved in return; when he only knows that he loves and is moving to its music—then, and then only, are two people able to dance perfectly in tune to the same rhythm.

But is this all to the relationship of the argonauta—this private pattern of two dancers perfectly in time? Should they not also be in tune with a larger rhythm, a natural swinging of the pendulum between sharing and solitude; between the intimate and the abstract; between the particular and the universal, the near and the far? And is it not the swinging of the pendulum between these opposite poles that makes a relationship nourishing? Yeats once said that the supreme experience of life was "to share profound thought and then to touch." But it takes both.

First touch, intimate touch of the personal and particular (the chores in the kitchen, the talk by the fire); then the loss of intimacy in the great stream of the impersonal and abstract (the silent beach, the bowl of stars overhead). Both partners are lost in a common sea of the universal which absorbs and yet frees, which separates and yet unites. Is this not what the more mature relationship, the meeting of two solitudes, is meant to be? The double-sunrise stage was only intimate and personal. The oyster bed was caught in the particular and the functional. But the argonauta, should they not be able to swing from the intimate and the particular and the functional out into the abstract and the universal, and then back to the personal again?

And in this image of the pendulum swinging in easy rhythm between opposite poles, is there not a clue to the problem of relationships as a whole? Is there not here even a hint of an understanding and an acceptance of the wingèd life of relationships, of their eternal ebb and flow, of their inevitable intermittency? . . .

Intermittency—an impossible lesson for human beings to learn. How can one learn to live through the ebb-tides of one's existence? How can one learn to take the trough of the wave? It is easier to understand here on the beach, where the breathlessly still ebb-tides reveal another life below the level which mortals usually reach. In this crystalline moment of suspense, one has a sudden revelation of the secret kingdom at the bottom of the sea. Here in the shallow flats one finds, wading through warm ripples, great horseconchs pivoting on a leg; white sand dollars, marble medallions engraved in mud; and myriads of bright-colored cochina-clams, glistening in the foam, their shells opening and shutting like butterflies' wings. So beautiful is the still hour of the sea's withdrawal, as beautiful as the sea's return when the encroaching waves pound up the beach, pressing to reach those dark rumpled chains of seaweed which mark the last high tide.

Perhaps this is the most important thing for me to take back from beach-living: simply the memory that each cycle of the tide is valid; each cycle of the wave is valid; each cycle of a relationship is valid. And my shells? I can sweep them all into my pocket. They are only there to remind me that the sea recedes and returns eternally.

a Comprehending the material

There are a few *words* that may cause you trouble. Be sure you look them up if they do, or you will miss just that much of the meaning of the passage. Do you know what a "coracle" is, for instance? It will help you to understand the light flimsy structure of the shell. How about "ebb-tide"? Don't confuse it with its opposite. And what does "crystalline moment of suspense" mean? If you are not familiar with the treasures of the beach you will have no clear image of "horse-conchs," "white sand dollars," "marble medallions," and "cochina-clams."

An understanding of the *allusions* in "Argonauta" is essential to comprehension. You will be more likely to realize the delicate fluting of the argonaut if you have seen pictures of a Greek column. More important though is the need to familiarize yourself with the Greek myth, the quest for the Golden Fleece by the Argonauts, for this quest is symbolic of the author's search for fulfillment in the "second half of life." It would be well, too, for you to know the sort of music Mozart wrote for country dances. It will give you a clearer understanding of the author's description of the dance.

You will find little trouble in comprehending the *syntax* of the lines. Anne Morrow Lindbergh writes very simply with a quiet even pace that seems to accompany the pace of her discoveries. It was necessary, however, for us to outline for you the *thought development* between Chapters I and VI not only because the author refers to the "shells," described in the intervening chapters, in her "Argonauta," but also because the imaginative framework of shells used throughout the book is redeveloped in summary form in this chapter. Knowing this will help you to understand that here the final answers to basic questions of life are being found.

Finally, although the achievements of Charles Lindbergh are universally known, it should be pointed out that his wife has a reputation in her own right. The daughter of a famous diplomat, she is widely traveled, an expert aviatrix, an author, and a mother. Knowing something of her background we can understand more precisely the reasons for her need to "get away from it all" for awhile. Maybe we will be encouraged to follow her example.

b   Reflecting upon the material

Not all of us can spend time at the seashore, but we all can escape briefly to some quiet place away from people and houses and stretch out prone becoming "like the elements on which one lies" and seeking—not digging—for some chance treasures of the spirit that will renew the spirit and will somehow set one right again. If we turn our imaginations loose for awhile we will find ourselves in tune with the musings of Anne Morrow Lindbergh and discover some of the gifts she discovered. Since this "getting in tune" is an imaginative process it is possible to accomplish this regardless of sex, regardless of age, and regardless of position. When we do get in tune, even partially, our appreciation of the selection will be enhanced.

The Argonauta is a contemplation on maturity in marriage. You will appreciate the author's thoughts better if you permit yourself to dwell on some of the images she describes: the swinging of a pendulum (preferably in a grandfather clock), the ebb and flow of the tide, and the light touchings and partings that occur in the country dance. Through such reflections you will gradually be able to relate these images to a pattern of living between two people that seems most conducive to happiness.

The reflective process may well take in an association of ideas from other readings. For example, Anne Morrow Lindbergh's comparison of the relationship between two people in a country dance to the relationship of husband and wife is similar to one created by Dorothy Sayers, the famous writer of mystery stories. She likened the marriage of her principal character, Lord Peter Wimsey, and his wife to the voices of a Bach fugue. Instead of the customary dominant role of the man and the corresponding submissive role of the woman (or vice versa) Miss Sayers would have the partners assume the role of the voices in the fugue, each one independent in melody but both interdependent in harmony.

An unhurried reflection will deepen your appreciation for *Gift from the Sea.*

V

PRESENTATION OF PROSE MATERIAL

> A man's discourse is like to a rich Persian carpet, the
> beautiful figures and patterns of which can be shown
> only by spreading and extending it out; when it is
> contracted and folded up, they are obscured and
> lost.
>
> JOHN DRYDEN

We have described the basic techniques required to clarify the
thought and reveal the feeling in all oral communication. Then
we have taken time to set up criteria that would be helpful in the
selection of worth-while material to read aloud, and we have
stressed the importance of the assimilation of that material before
reading aloud to others. We are now concerned with the problem
of applying the basic techniques of oral reading to the particular
selection read so that an audience may share fully in the reader's
appreciation.

1 PATTERNS OF INTERPRETATION

It is the responsibility of the oral reader to plan a pattern of
interpretation that will be a close facsimile of the written material.
We cannot stress too much the importance of *total communication*
if your audience is to get from you what you have got from the
material read. This necessitates a focus of attention on an oral
interpretation that will reproduce for your listeners the *total selection* in whole and in part. In other words, the oral reading should
match the written material.

To prepare an adequate reading pattern the first step will be
to make a complete analysis of your selection. This will have been
done in large measure in the process of assimilation as discussed
in the last chapter. Your next step will be to decide just how you
are to prepare an interpretative pattern that will reveal the results

of your analysis. Just how will you make the progression from one idea, or mood, or sentiment to another? How will you build up to and recede from a climax? How will you reveal shifts in action, emotional intensity, characterizations? How will you introduce echoes of previous thoughts, repetitions, refrains? How will you compare or contrast?

To answer these questions will require no new disciplines or tactics. You need merely to apply the basic techniques with which you are already familiar. Previously these techniques were studied from the point of view of making an accurate vocal reproduction of one particular thought or feeling, but now, when it is your intention to read an entire selection, you must apply these techniques so that in addition to each separate detail you can reproduce the sequence of thoughts and feelings and their interrelationships.

At the risk of oversimplification we might suggest that in preparing a pattern of the whole your major task will consist of planning suitable variations. Each thought unfolded differs slightly or moderately or considerably from the one preceding it. So does each mood, each feeling, each episode. On the other hand there may be a return to a theme previously introduced. If so you must decide how nearly your pattern of interpretation will resemble the original. In short your task will be to decide when to vary the vocal factors of oral communication (especially the factors of tempo, intensity, and quality) and when to keep them relatively constant. This cannot be an arbitrary decision but must stem from your analysis of the material.

Your last step is practicing out loud. Some, who have access to a tape recorder, prefer to make a tape recording. Some need the presence of another person to give reactions and to offer suggestions. Others prefer to read aloud in privacy. Whatever the means, the end should be oral rehearsal, for, if it is not, the chances are you will be practicing silent rather than oral reading. Don't stop until you have done your best. You may need to practice one line many times over.

The more considered your analysis, the more control you have over voice and body, the more accurate will be your pattern of interpretation, and the more successful will be your presentation of what the author has written.

We will now submit some studies in the interpretation of some major literary forms, prose in this chapter and poetry in the next. For each selection we will include the full text and a suggested pattern of interpretation which should be of help to you if you should choose to read it. We have endeavored to leave many decisions up to you, for, as we have so often said, there is no one "right" interpretation.

For each reading you undertake (and it would appear desirable for you to have the experience of reading several types of literature) your basic preparation should be the same: select wisely, assimilate thoroughly, and then, with adequate facility in utilizing the basic techniques of oral communication, prepare a detailed pattern of interpretation that will enable you to share your enjoyment of your selection with others.

2 STUDIES IN READING PROSE

a Stately prose

The Gettysburg Address

Four score and seven years ago our fathers brought forth upon this continent a new nation, conceived in liberty and dedicated to the proposition that all men are created equal. Now we are engaged in a great civil war, testing whether that nation or any nation so conceived and so dedicated can long endure. We are met on a great battlefield of that war. We are met to dedicate a portion of it as the final resting place of those who here gave their lives that that nation might live. It is altogether fitting and proper that we should do this.

But in a larger sense we cannot dedicate, we cannot consecrate, we cannot hallow this ground. The brave men living and dead, who struggled here have consecrated it far above our power to add or detract. The world will little note nor long remember what we say here, but it can never forget what they did here. It is for us, the living, rather to be dedicated here to the unfinished work that they have thus far so nobly carried on. It is rather for us to be here dedicated to the great task remaining before us, that from these honored dead we take increased devotion to that cause for which they here gave the last full measure of devotion; that we here highly resolve that the dead shall not have died in vain; that the nation shall, under God, have a new birth of freedom, and that government of the people, by the people, and for the people shall not perish from the earth.

Suggested interpretation

The basic structure is very simple, consisting of three parts: (1) why we have come here, (2) what we cannot do, (3) what we can do. Any thoughtful oral interpretation should bring these parts into focus; otherwise the reading will obscure the message. The intent may be to convey the impression of dignity, sorrow, and earnest resolution, but unless the basic thoughts are set forth clearly, somnolence might prevail over understanding.

How are these three leading ideas presented? Simply by pushing them to the fore. The first two ideas might be clearly distinguished by a pattern in which a different pitch level, a slightly different tempo, or a different quality of voice (reflective of a different attitude) is employed when you come to the words: "But in a larger sense . . ." It is important that the contrast between what we cannot do and what we can do, so clearly expressed by Lincoln, is made sharply. The final resolution: "Let us here highly resolve . . ." is, of course, in the nature of a prayer. The tempo should be slower, the quality more spiritual, and the intensity more even.

There is a pleasing sound sequence in the address created partially by a slight variation in the movement of successive phrases and sentences. How should the voice reveal this cadence? Should the repetitive words be picked up with exactly the same tempo, intensity, and quality?

There are two repetitive constructions in the address:

> We cannot dedicate, we cannot consecrate, we cannot hallow this ground

and

> that government of the people, by the people, and for the people . . .

It might not be important to strive for a similar effect in reading each series, but it might be a subtle means of pleasing the ear.

The more practical problem concerns the use of stress to clarify
the thought. Should "we" or "cannot" or "dedicate" be stressed,
or two of the words, or all three? Similarly, should "of" or
"people" or both be stressed? You must grasp the basic meaning.
When you do, and when your decision is right, the sound sequence
in these two lines will be satisfying.

There is no better illustration in literature of matter and manner
being so happily blended.

b Biblical prose

Ecclesiasticus XLIII

The pride of the height, the clear firmament, the beauty of heaven,
with his glorious shew;

2   The sun when it appeareth, declaring at his rising a marvellous
instrument, the work of the most High:

3   At noon it parcheth the country, and who can abide the burning heat thereof?

4   A man blowing a furnace is in works of heat, but the sun
burneth the mountains three times more; breathing out fiery va-
pours, and sending forth bright beams, it dimmeth the eyes.

5   Great is the Lord that made it; and at his commandment it
runneth hastily.

6   He made the moon also to serve in her season for a declaration
of times, and a sign of the world.

7   From the moon is the sign of feasts, a light that decreaseth in
her perfection.

8   The month is called after her name, increasing wonderfully in
her changing, being an instrument of the armies above, shining in
the firmament of heaven;

9   The beauty of heaven, the glory of the stars, an ornament giving light in the highest places of the Lord.

10   At the commandment of the Holy One they will stand in their
order, and never faint in their watches.

11   Look upon the rainbow, and praise him that made it; very
beautiful it is in the brightness thereof.

12   It compasseth the heaven about with a glorious circle, and the hands of the most High have bended it.

13   By his commandment he maketh the snow to fall apace, and sendeth swiftly the lightnings of his judgment.

14   Through this the treasures are opened: and clouds fly forth as fowls.

15   By his great power he maketh the clouds firm, and the hailstones are broken small.

16   At his sight the mountains are shaken, and at his will the south wind bloweth.

17   The noise of the thunder maketh the earth to tremble: so doth the northern storm and the whirlwind: as birds flying he scattereth the snow, and the falling down thereof is as the lighting of grasshoppers:

18   The eye marvelleth at the beauty of the whiteness thereof, and the heart is astonished at the raining of it.

19   The hoarfrost also as salt he poureth on the earth, and being congealed, it lieth on the top of sharp stakes.

20   When the cold north wind bloweth, and the water is congealed into ice, it abideth upon every gathering together of water, and clotheth the water as with a breastplate.

21   It devoureth the mountains, and burneth the wilderness, and consumeth the grass as fire.

22   A present remedy of all is a mist coming speedily: a dew coming after heat refresheth.

23   By his counsel he appeaseth the deep, and planteth islands therein.

24   They that sail on the sea tell of the danger thereof; and when we hear it with our ears, we marvel thereat.

25   For therein be strange and wondrous works, variety of all kinds of beasts and whales created.

26   By him the end of them hath prosperous success, and by his word all things consist.

27   We may speak much, and yet come short: wherefore in sum, he is all.

28 How shall we be able to magnify him? for he is great above all his works.

29 The Lord is terrible and very great, and marvellous in his power.

30 When ye glorify the Lord, exalt him as much as ye can; for even yet will he far exceed: and when ye exalt him, put forth all your strength, and be not weary; for ye can never go far enough.

31 Who hath seen him, that he might tell us? and who can magnify him as he is?

32 There are yet hid greater things than these be, for we have seen but a few of his works.

33 For the Lord hath made all things; and to the godly hath he given wisdom.

Suggested interpretation

There are some passages from the Bible, such as this one, that may very well be classified as poetry. The rhythmic cadence is almost metrical. Imagery is used in compressed abundance. It may rightly be called poetry, as might some of the speeches of Lincoln or Churchill. Yet there are prayers as imaginative, and they are prose; and the form is prose rather than poetic. Whatever the classification, this is beautiful in content and form and can be read magnificently.

The basic structure is the simple progression of the objects of creation presented one after another for description and praise, beginning in the heavens and ending on the earth. No one of these is necessarily more wonderful or beautiful than another. There is, therefore, no necessity to build to a climax. The climax, verse 27, is achieved by the summation alone: the works of God are so many and all so wonderful.

Whether one holds to a literal or to a liberal interpretation of the Bible, whether he belongs to a particular religious sect or holds himself independent of sects, whether he takes a deistic or a pantheistic view of creation, he can still appreciate the solemnity, the grandeur, and the simplicity of this passage. The basic mood is awe and reverence; and this need not be strained or feigned.

There should probably be pauses of different lengths to separate the major groupings from each other and to separate the objects within each group. There are full open sounds throughout. Giving them adequate duration of utterance will enhance the effect of awe and wonder. And since reverence and awe prevail, suitable feeling tones should be produced to reveal this mood.

You will notice the more detailed and refined relationships as you study each separate verse. Prepare an interpretation to fit each one. You need not strive for effect; the form is quite simple. The beauty of the chapter lies in this simplicity. You will notice among other things, however, that there is a rhythmic balance achieved in nearly every verse, usually pivoted on the word *and*. What sort of interpretation will express this balance? Will the second half be an echo of the first? Will the one build in intensity and the other diminish? Will the balance be made more prominent here, less so there, and ignored altogether elsewhere?

And how will you read the words "He is all" (verse 29)? What comes before leads up to that. What follows is by way of an epilogue.

c   Informal prose

What's Wrong with the Comics?

THE ATTACK: JOHN MASON BROWN
THE DEFENSE: AL CAPP *

JOHN MASON BROWN

The comics, alas, like death and taxes, are very much with us and to my way of thinking they are equally unfunny. Why they are called comics when people who read them, young and old, always look like so many undertakers during the reading, eludes me. But we'll let that pass, just as most of us parents have had   5 to let comics pass into our homes, against our will, against our wishes, against our better judgment.

I love comedians, the highest, the lowest, and the toughest, and I love cartoons, too, but my allergy to comics is complete, utter, absolute. I *know* there are bad comics and I am *told* there are   10 good comics. I have read them—a few of both, only a few, for-

* Town Meeting of the Air, March 2, 1948 (Town Meeting Bulletin, Vol. 13, #45). Reprinted by permission of Town Hall—A Division of New York University.

tunately—under protest, but I regret them both. I deplore them and, to continue the understatement, I abhor them.

So far as I am concerned, they might just as well be written in a foreign language for which no dictionary has ever been published, and I wish they had been.

Let me quickly admit that I am low enough and sometimes defeated enough as a parent to make use of comics. I mean in desperate moments when, of a rainy Sunday morning or afternoon, I want peace in the home. Or when I'm traveling with my two sons on a train and I need to subdue them. Then—yes, I'll confess it —I do resort to comics, without shame, without conscience.

On such occasions, I don't so much distribute comics as I administer them to my sons, much as a barkeep would pour out Mickey Finns or a doctor distribute hypodermics. As knock-out drops for unruly children, as sedatives, as Maxim silencers comics do have their undeniable uses. This much I'll concede gratefully.

I also grant that so long as other people's children read comics, we have scant hope, and perhaps less right, to keep ours from doing so. It would be unfair for us to deny to our children what is now a group experience and when they have grown up will have become a group memory for their generation.

If I hate the comics, I promise you I have my reasons for doing so. I know that as part of every healthy diet, everyone needs a certain amount of trash. Each generation has always found its own. The comic books, however, as they are nowadays perpetually on tap, seem to me not only to be trash but the lowest, most despicable, and most harmful and unethical form of trash.

As a rule, their word selection is as wretched as their drawings or the paper on which they are printed. They are designed for readers who are too lazy to read and who don't want to read anyway.

I won't and can't deny that comic books fascinate the young as, in terms of pigs, rabbits, rodents, morons, hillbillies, and supermen, they tell their illustrated stories. But as a writer, I resent the way in which they get along with the poorest kind of writing. I hate their lack of style! I hate their appeal to illiterate literates!

I loathe their bad grammar, their tiresome toughness, their cheap thrills, and their imbecilic laughter!

I hate them for making only the story count and not the how of its telling. I detest them in spite of their alleged thrills and gags because they have no subtlety and certainly no beauty. Their power of seduction, I believe, lies in the fact that they make everything too easy.

They substitute bad drawing for good description. They reduce the wonders of the language to crude monosyllables and to narratives which are really nothing but printed motion pictures.

What riles me when I see my children absorbed by the comics is my awareness of what they are not reading and could be reading; in other words, of the more genuine and deeper pleasures they could and should be having.

To compare Bugs Bunny or Donald Duck with the *Jungle Book* or even the *Travels of Babar,* and to set Wanda the Wonder Woman against *Alice in Wonderland,* or Batman and Robin, Dick Tracy, and Gene Autry against *Treasure Island,* or Li'l Abner, if Mr. Capp will forgive me, against Huck Finn or Tom Sawyer, or Superman and Captain Marvel against Jules Verne or *Gulliver's Travels* is to realize that between the modern cave drawing—which a comic book really is—and a real book, a good book, there is, to put it mildly, a difference, a tragic difference which is hard on the young and may be harder on the future.

Anatole France once described even the best books as being the opium of the Occident. Well, most comics, as I see them are the marijuana of the nursery! They are the bane of the bassinet! They are the horror of the home, the curse of the kids, and a threat to the future!

The comics offer final and melancholy proof that even among the young the mind is the most unused muscle in the United States.

AL CAPP

There must have been a lot of innocent little kids who listened and I'm sure they were frightened to death listening to Mr. Brown tell them what's wrong with their comics.

I'd like to hear a Town Hall forum of the same kids on the subject, "What's Wrong with Dramatic Critics?" They might, with complete righteousness, make the same complaints about dramatic critics that Mr. Brown makes about comic strips like, for instance "Dramatic critics are a waste of time." "Dramatic critics are very unfunny; they're bad for the eyes; they're untrue to life; they're horrible to think about." "Dramatic critics are not only the bane of the bassinet, they're the didey service of the nursery."

Of course, as any fool can plainly see, these kids would be wrong, because kids just aren't the best judges of dramatic critics. And this point occurred to me during Mr. Brown's speech; dramatic critics just aren't the best judges of kids.

This whole thing gives me an idea for one of my own contributions to juvenile delinquency, which I call rather defiantly my comic strip. The scene is a typical American home of a typical American family named Kinsey, of course.

Supper is over and seated in the living room are Mr. and Mrs. Kinsey and their eleven-year-old son, Kingsblood. They're discussing what they read in that day's typical American newspaper.

Mr. Kinsey says he's mighty pleased about the new atomic bomb which can blast the bloody brains out of two or three hundred million irritating foreigners.

Then he chats about the prizefight in Chicago that resulted in one of the young athletes being punched to death in front of thousands of happy, cheering, typical American sports lovers.

But Mrs. Kinsey is more interested in talking about the latest society divorce and the front page excerpts from the fun-loving young matron's diary in which she refers with fine, wholesome frankness to her dates with twenty or thirty of her husband's dipsomaniac chums. Well, Kingsblood has gone through all that, and frankly it bored him. He's reading the one page of the family newspaper where there's real action—the comic page.

Mrs. Kinsey, noticing that little Kingsblood isn't joining in this uplifting discussion of the front page of their family newspaper, glances over his shoulder and screams a typical, horrified, American mother-type scream.

"Look," she screams at Mr. Kinsey, "look at what your child   40
is reading."

"It's only Dick Gravy," replies little Kingsblood. (I am referring
here to a certain detective comic strip which shall remain name-
less, because I'm too shrewd to give a rival all this valuable pub-
licity.)   45

"Only Dick Gravy, my eye," snarls his mother. "Why this thing
is full of murder, crime, violence, and look, why there's even a
boy in it who doesn't think that a girl in it is repulsive so it's full
of S-E-X, too."

Mr. Kinsey speaks, "Yes, I've been reading several articles lately   50
by several psychologists, or psychiatrists, or something, that state
that these stories of murder, crime, violence and S-E-X are very
bad stuff for kids."

He says, "Why do you bother with that old comic page, anyhow, son? Why don't you read the news?"   55

"I did, Pop," replies the lad, "And oh, boy, it's all full of murder, and crime, and violence, and S-E-X too, Pop."

Mr. Kinsey looks over the front page of the paper and he has
to admit that the kid is right. He tears the newspaper up, cancels
his subscription, and he says, "Then according to those articles   60
by those critics and psychologists, news is bad stuff for kids. Those
psychologists must be right, because all the articles about psychologists all say they're always right, and those articles must be right
because they're written by other psychologists."

"Son," Mr. Kinsey said, pulling a volume off the bookshelf,   65
"why don't you read a good book instead, like *Oliver Twist?*"

"I read it," reports little Kinsey. "It's about a kid who falls in
with a criminal named Fagin who teaches him how to commit
crimes. There's a big gorilla in it, named Sikes, who beats a girl
to death."   70

"Stop," cries his father. "Stop! I can see now that the work of
Charles Dickens is very bad for kids." So he tears the works of
Dickens all up. He feels he owes this to the psychologists.

Now, Mr. Kinsey, with all those articles by the psychologists in
his mind, goes through his typical American family bookshelf.   75

He re-examines *Treasure Island* and *Kidnapped* by Robert Louis Stevenson and he finds several very deplorable murders and lots of rip-roaring crime and violence in them, and he tears them all up.

He's very tired by this time. *Alice in Wonderland* has got to go because the Queen in that keeps saying, "Off with their heads!" 80 and that's not only violent, but it often results in death.

Well, pretty soon there's nothing left in the house except a phone book and a volume of Shakespeare. With a sigh, little Kingsblood picks up the volume of Shakespeare and begins to read.

With a loud roar of "No, no, no, my child!" his father snatches 85 it away from him in the nick of time. "This book is full of stories of murder, crime, violence, and S-E-X!" he roars.

"But, Pop," whimpered little Kingsblood, "It's Shakespeare!"

"Fancy names don't fool me," replies his father. "I've read those articles by those critics and psychologists. If they are right, 90 Shakespeare is poison for kids. If they're right, Shakespeare is a very bad influence."

Now, comic strips are nothing new. They are as old a form as the written word itself. They are just combinations of pictures and text which tell stories. The Egyptians did them in their own way 95 in the tombs of the Pharaohs. [We] do them now in our own way.

Comic strippers are story tellers, just the same as people who write radio shows, books, and movies. Some of us are right and some of us are wrong. It's the same with psychologists—and even dramatic critics. Some of them are right, some are wrong. But 100 don't worry about the kids. They're usually right.

Suggested interpretation

This debate has been selected not only because an audience always enjoys a real clash of opinion on a subject of considerable concern to young and old alike, but because there is a clash of personalities and style as well. Brown proceeds with lightning rapid thrusts of his verbal rapier to attack the comics not for their immorality but for their inanity. His figures are brilliant, his wit is sparkling. Capp proceeds with leisurely deviltry to cast his entire case in the framework of a verbal comic strip—a brilliant imaginative technique. Brown attacks with good-humored venom; Capp defends with hilarious ridicule.

In the light of the foregoing analysis should not your interpretation reveal this contrast of personality and technique? If so, then probably the average tempo and intensity with which each is read should be clearly distinguished. The element of quality merits consideration. Can you manage a feeling tone of disdain, superiority, and amusement for Brown and one of disarming informality, mock melodrama (in places) and, possibly, smugness for Capp?

How would you work out the basic sequence of each speech? Where do the leading ideas begin and end, and how would you reveal these changes to your listeners—by change of pace, pause, eye contact, change of quality, or what?

There are, of course, innumerable detailed problems of interpretation to work out. We will point to but a few.

In Brown's speech notice, for example, his technique of emphasizing a point by a repetition of like sounds or like syntactical structures arranged in short, rapid sequence. ". . . against our will, against our wishes, against our better judgment (lines 6-7), . . . "the highest, the lowest, and the toughest . . . complete, utter, absolute" (8-10), "I deplore them, . . . I abhor them" (12-13) . . . "without shame, without conscience" (22) are but a few. If this technique is employed for emphasis, how will you handle it when you read aloud?

There is an opportunity to show by contrast in quality (and possibly in duration) the relative worth of the selections listed as examples of the good and the bad (62-71).

Finally, how would you interpret the last two paragraphs? Would there be a sudden shift in tempo and intensity beginning with "marijuana of the nursery!"? And, be careful that you let the laughs die down (there should be some) before you read the last paragraph. Don't forget the very last line must indicate both finality and triumph.

The use of pause for effect is very important in Capp's speech. Also, a fine sense of timing is required. The very quietness and "sanity" of the first sentence, in contrast to Brown's brilliant intensity, should be most effective. Then a sudden shift to imitate Brown's tempo and intensity (lines 8-10), followed by a vocal trumping of Brown's ace, "the bane of the bassinet" with "the didey service of the nursery" could prove to be an unmitigated delight if your pattern is well made.

Would you pause for effect before "Kinsey" (19) and before "Kingsblood" (21)?

Consider the line ". . . screams a typical, horrified, American mother-type scream" (38-39). How will you read this—straight, with mock terror, with exaggerated restraint, as a scream, or with coyness?

How are you going to read "S-E-X" each time it appears?

Will the last paragraph of the speech recapture the slow drawl of the first paragraph?

The details of interpretation are important in Capp's speech. He talks with his tongue in one cheek before his "skit," the tongue in the other cheek during the skit, but he becomes straightforward and forceful at the end.

You really should enjoy this reading.

d Narrative prose

The Night the Bed Fell

JAMES THURBER *

I suppose that the high-water mark of my youth in Columbus, Ohio, was the night the bed fell on my father. It makes a better recitation (unless as some friends of mine have said, one has heard it five or six times) than it does a piece of writing, for it is almost necessary to throw furniture around, shake doors, and bark like a dog, to lend the proper atmosphere and verisimilitude to what is admittedly a somewhat incredible tale. Still, it did take place.

It happened, then, that my father had decided to sleep in the attic one night, to be away where he could think. My mother opposed the notion strongly because, she said, the old wooden bed up there was unsafe; it was wobbly and the heavy headboard would crash down on father's head in case the bed fell, and kill him. There was no dissuading him, however, and at a quarter past ten he closed the attic door behind him and went up the narrow twisting stairs. We later heard ominous creakings as he crawled into bed. Grandfather, who usually slept in the attic bed when he was with us, had disappeared some days before. (On these occasions he usually was gone six or eight days and returned growling and out of temper, with the news that the Federal Union was run by a passel of blockheads and that the Army of the Potomac didn't have any more chance than a fiddler's bitch.)

We had visiting us at this time a nervous first cousin of mine named Briggs Beall, who believed that he was likely to cease breathing when he was asleep. It was his feeling that if he were not awakened every hour during the night, he might die of suffocation. He had been accustomed to setting an alarm clock to ring at intervals until morning, but I persuaded him to abandon this. He slept in my room and I told him that I was such a light sleeper that if anybody quit breathing in the same room with me, I would wake instantly. He tested me the first night—which I had suspected he would—by holding his breath after my regular breathing had convinced him I was asleep. I was not asleep, however, and called to him. This seemed to allay his fears a little, but he took the precaution of putting a glass of spirits of camphor on a little table at the head of his bed. In case I didn't arouse him until he was almost gone, he said, he would sniff the camphor, a powerful reviver. Briggs was not the only member of his family who had his crotchets. Old Aunt Melissa Beall (who could whistle like a man, with two fingers in her mouth) suffered under the premonition that she was destined to die on South High Street because she had been born on South High Street and married on South High Street. Then there was Aunt Sarah Shoaf, who never went to bed at night without the fear that a burglar was going to get in and blow chloroform under her door through a tube. To avert this calamity—for she was in greater dread of anesthetics than of losing her household goods—she always piled her money, silverware, and other valuables in a neat stack just outside her bedroom with a note reading: "This is all I have. Please take it and do not use your chloroform, as this is all I have." Aunt Gracie Shoaf also had a burglar phobia, but she met it with more fortitude. She was

confident that burglars had been getting into her house every night
for forty years. The fact that she never missed anything was to her
no proof to the contrary. She always claimed that she scared them
off before they could take anything, by throwing shoes down the
hallway. When she went to bed she piled, where she could get to
them handily, all the shoes there were about her house. Five minutes after she had turned off the light, she would sit up in bed and
say "Hark!" Her husband, who had learned to ignore the whole situation as long ago as 1903, would either be sound asleep or pretend
to be sound asleep. In either case he would not respond to her
tugging and pulling, so that presently she would arise, tiptoe to
the door, open it slightly and heave a shoe down the hall in one
direction and its mate down the hall in the other direction. Some
nights she threw them all, some nights only a couple of pair.

But I am straying from the remarkable incidents that took place
during the night that the bed fell on father. By midnight we were
all in bed. The layout of the rooms and the disposition of their
occupants is important to an understanding of what later occurred.
In the front room upstairs (just under father's attic bedroom)
were my mother and my brother Herman, who sometimes sang in
his sleep, usually "Marching Through Georgia" or "Onward, Christian Soldiers." Briggs Beall and myself were in a room adjoining
this one. My brother Roy was in a room across the hall from ours.
Our bull terrier, Rex, slept in the hall.

My bed was an army cot, one of those affairs which are made
wide enough to sleep on comfortable only by putting up, flat with
the middle section, the two sides which ordinarily hang down like
the sideboards of a drop-leaf table. When these sides are up, it is
perilous to roll too far toward the edge, for then the cot is likely
to tip completely over, bringing the whole bed down on top of
one, with a tremendous banging crash. This, in fact, is precisely
what happened, about two o'clock in the morning. (It was my
mother who, in recalling the scene later, first referred to it as "the
night the bed fell on your father.")

Always a deep sleeper, slow to arouse (I had lied to Briggs),

I was at first unconscious of what had happened when the iron cot rolled me onto the floor and toppled over on me. It left me still warmly bundled up and unhurt, for the bed rested above me like a canopy. Hence I did not wake up, only reached the edge of consciousness and went back. The racket, however, instantly awakened my mother, in the next room, who came to the immediate conclusion that her worst dread was realized: the big wooden bed upstairs had fallen on father. She therefore screamed, "Let's go to your poor father!" It was this shout, rather than the noise of my cot falling, that awakened my brother Herman, in the same room with her. He thought that mother had become, for no apparent reason, hysterical. "You're all right, mamma!" he shouted, trying to calm her. They exchanged shout for shout for perhaps ten seconds: "Let's go to your poor father!" and "You're all right!" That woke up Briggs. By this time I was conscious of what was going on, in a vague way, but did not yet realize that I was under my bed instead of on it. Briggs, awakening in the midst of loud shouts of fear and apprehension, came to the quick conclusion that he was suffocating and that we were all trying to "bring him out." With a low moan, he grasped the glass of camphor at the head of his bed and instead of sniffing it poured it over himself. The room reeked of camphor. "Ugf, ahfg!" choked Briggs, like a drowning man, for he had almost succeeded in stopping his breath under the deluge of pungent spirits. He leaped out of bed and groped toward the open window, but he came up against one that was closed. With his hand, he beat out the glass, and I could hear it crash and tinkle in the alleyway below. It was at this juncture that I, in trying to get up, had the uncanny sensation of feeling my bed above me! Foggy with sleep, I now suspected, in my turn, that the whole uproar was being made in a frantic endeavor to extricate me from what must be an unheard-of and perilous situation. "Get me out of this!" I bawled. "Get me out!" I think I had the nightmarish belief that I was entombed in a mine. "Gugh," gasped Briggs, floundering in his camphor.

By this time my mother, still shouting, pursued by Herman,

still shouting, was trying to open the door to the attic, in order to go up and get my father's body out of the wreckage. The door was stuck, however, and wouldn't yield. Her frantic pulls on it only added to the general banging and confusion. Roy and the dog were now up, the one shouting questions, the other barking.

Father, farthest away and soundest sleeper of all, had by this time been awakened by the battering on the attic door. He decided that the house was on fire. "I'm coming, I'm coming!" he wailed in a slow sleepy voice—it took him many minutes to regain full consciousness. My mother, still believing he was caught under the bed, detected in his "I'm coming!" the mournful, resigned note of one who is preparing to meet his Maker. "He's dying!" she shouted.

"I'm all right!" Briggs yelled, to reassure her. "I'm all right!" He still believed that it was his own closeness to death that was worrying mother. I found at last the light switch in my room, unlocked the door, and Briggs and I joined the others at the attic door. The dog, who never did like Briggs, jumped for him— assuming that he was the culprit in whatever was going on—and Roy had to throw Rex and hold him. We could hear father crawling out of bed upstairs. Roy pulled the attic door open, with a mighty jerk, and father came down the stairs, sleepy and irritable but safe and sound. My mother began to weep when she saw him. Rex began to howl. "What in the name of God is going on here?" asked father.

The situation was finally put together like a gigantic jigsaw puzzle. Father caught a cold from prowling around in his bare feet but there were no other bad results. "I'm glad," said mother, who always looked on the bright side of things, "that your grandfather wasn't here."

Suggested interpretation

There is no better entertainment than a Thurber story or reminiscence. Thurber uses bold strokes but they are true and they strike deep. Human foibles are exaggerated so they can be spotted and laughed at. If bold strokes predominate in the writing, they should predominate in the reading. Your basic interpretation should be straight, direct, and rapid moving.

The story is rather long, and you may find it desirable or necessary to cut. If so, you should first read the selection several times to yourself until the main parts in the development of the plot as well as the different characters depicted fit into place. Developing such a familiarity with the story makes it possible to cut judiciously without destroying the established movement of the sequence and also to maintain consistent character interpretation. Such an operation can be followed in cutting any prose or narrative poetry selection. It is always possible, too, to cut more radically by relating omitted sequences in your own words.

Variation is important in any relatively long selection, or attention will lag. You must not, of course, vary tempo, intensity, etc., just for the sake of variety, but if you are thoroughly familiar with the relationship of part to part you can take advantage of the opportunity, when it presents itself, to create a varied pattern.

You will find one problem to solve: the maintenance of consistent characterizations for the several characters in describing their movements and in reading their lines. You need not (probably should not) impersonate. Suggestion is sufficient. But once you have found a satisfying vocal pattern for each character, practice until you can reproduce it at will.

e   A play

Hello Out There

WILLIAM SAROYAN *

There is a fellow in a small-town prison cell, tapping slowly on the floor with a spoon. After tapping half a minute, as if he were trying to telegraph words, he gets up and begins walking around the cell. At last he stops, stands at the center of the cell, and doesn't move for a long time. He feels his head, as if it were wounded. Then he looks around. Then he calls out dramatically, kidding the world.

* From *Razzle-Dazzle* by William Saroyan. Reprinted by permission of the author.

YOUNG MAN	Hello—out there! (Pause) Hello—out there! Hello—out there! (Long pause) Nobody out there. (Still more dramatically, but more comically, too) Hello—out there! Hello—out there!

(A girl's voice is heard, very sweet and soft.)

THE VOICE	Hello.
YOUNG MAN	Hello—out there.
THE VOICE	Hello.
YOUNG MAN	Is that you, Katey?
THE VOICE	No—this here is Emily.
YOUNG MAN	Who? (*Swiftly*) Hello out there.
THE VOICE	Emily.
YOUNG MAN	Emily who? I don't know anybody named Emily. Are you that girl I met at Sam's in Salinas about three years ago?
THE VOICE	No—I'm the girl who cooks here. I'm the cook. I've never been in Salinas. I don't even know where it is.
YOUNG MAN	Hello out there. You say you cook here?
THE VOICE	Yes.
YOUNG MAN	Well, why don't you study up and learn to cook? How come I don't get no jello or anything good?
THE VOICE	I just cook what they tell me to. (*Pause*) You lonesome?
YOUNG MAN	Lonesome as a coyote. Hear me hollering? Hello out there!
THE VOICE	Who you hollering to?
YOUNG MAN	Well—nobody, I guess. I been trying to think of somebody to write a letter to, but I can't think of anybody.
THE VOICE	What about Katey?
YOUNG MAN	I don't know anybody named Katey.
THE VOICE	Then why did you say is that you, Katey?
YOUNG MAN	Katey's a good name. I always did like a name

	like Katey. I never *knew* anybody named Katey, though.
THE VOICE	*I* did.
YOUNG MAN	Yeah? What was she like? Tall girl, or little one?
THE VOICE	Kind of medium.
YOUNG MAN	Hello out there. What sort of a looking girl are *you?*
THE VOICE	Oh, I don't know.
YOUNG MAN	Didn't anybody ever tell you? Didn't anybody ever talk to you that way?
THE VOICE	What way?
YOUNG MAN	You know. Didn't they?
THE VOICE	No, they didn't.
YOUNG MAN	Ah, the fools—they should have. I can tell from your voice you're O.K.
THE VOICE	Maybe I am and maybe I ain't.
YOUNG MAN	I never missed yet.
THE VOICE	Yeah, I know. That's why you're in jail.
YOUNG MAN	The whole thing was a mistake.
THE VOICE	They claim it was rape.
YOUNG MAN	No—it wasn't.
THE VOICE	That's what they claim it was.
YOUNG MAN	They're a lot of fools.
THE VOICE	Well, you sure are in trouble. Are you scared?
YOUNG MAN	Scared to death. (*Suddenly*) Hello out there!
THE VOICE	What do you keep saying that for all the time?
YOUNG MAN	I'm lonesome. I'm as lonesome as a coyote. (*A long one*) Hello—out there!

(*The Girl appears, over to one side. She is a plain girl in plain clothes.*)

THE GIRL	I'm kind of lonesome, too.
YOUNG MAN	(*Turning and looking at her*) Hey—no fooling? Are you?
THE GIRL	Yeah—I'm almost as lonesome as a coyote myself.

YOUNG MAN	Who *you* lonesome for?
THE GIRL	I don't know.
YOUNG MAN	It's the same with me. The minute they put you in a place like this you remember all the girls you ever knew, and all the girls you didn't get to know, and it sure gets lonesome.
THE GIRL	I bet it does.
YOUNG MAN	Ah, it's awful. (*Pause*) You're a pretty kid, you know that?
THE GIRL	You're just talking.
YOUNG MAN	No, I'm not just talking—you *are* pretty. Any fool could see that. You're just about the prettiest kid in the whole world.
THE GIRL	I'm not—and you know it.
YOUNG MAN	No—you are. I never saw anyone prettier in all my born days, in all my travels. I knew Texas would bring me luck.
THE GIRL	Luck? You're in jail, aren't you? You've got a whole gang of people all worked up, haven't you?
YOUNG MAN	Ah, that's nothing, I'll get out of this.
THE GIRL	Maybe.
YOUNG MAN	No, I'll be all right—*now*.
THE GIRL	What do you mean—now?
YOUNG MAN	I mean after seeing you. I got something now. You know for a while there I didn't care one way or another. Tired. (*Pause*) Tired of trying for the best all the time and never getting it. (*Suddenly*) Hello out there!
THE GIRL	Who are you calling now?
YOUNG MAN	You.
THE GIRL	Why, I'm right here.
YOUNG MAN	I know. (*Calling*) Hello out there!
THE GIRL	Hello.
YOUNG MAN	Ah, you're sweet. (*Pause*) I'm going to marry *you*. I'm going away with *you*. I'm going to take

	you to San Francisco or some place like that. I *am,* now. I'm going to win myself some real money, too. I'm going to study 'em real careful and pick myself some winners, and we're going to have a lot of money.
THE GIRL	Yeah?
YOUNG MAN	Yeah. Tell me your name and all that stuff.
THE GIRL	Emily.
YOUNG MAN	I know that. What's the rest of it? Where were you born? Come on, tell me the whole thing.
THE GIRL	Emily Smith.
YOUNG MAN	Honest to God?
THE GIRL	Honest. That's my name—Emily Smith.
YOUNG MAN	Ah, you're the sweetest girl in the whole world.
THE GIRL	Why?
YOUNG MAN	I don't know why, but you are, that's all. Where were you born?
THE GIRL	Matador, Texas.
YOUNG MAN	Where's that?
THE GIRL	Right here.
YOUNG MAN	Is this Matador, Texas?
THE GIRL	Yeah, it's Matador. They brought you here from Wheeling.
YOUNG MAN	Is that where I was—Wheeling?
THE GIRL	Didn't you even know what town you were in?
YOUNG MAN	All towns are alike. You don't go up and ask somebody what town you're in. It doesn't make any difference. How far away is Wheeling?
THE GIRL	Sixteen or seventeen miles. Didn't you know they moved you?
YOUNG MAN	How could I know, when I was out—cold? Somebody hit me over the head with a lead pipe or something. What'd they hit me for?
THE GIRL	Rape—that's what they *said.*
YOUNG MAN	Ah, that's a lie. (*Amazed, almost to himself*) She wanted me to give her money.

THE GIRL	Money?
YOUNG MAN	Yeah, if I'd have known she was a woman like that—well, by God, I'd have gone on down the street and stretched out in a park somewhere and gone to sleep.
THE GIRL	Is that what she wanted—money?
YOUNG MAN	Yeah. A fellow like me hopping freights all over the country, trying to break his bad luck, going from one poor little town to another, trying to get in on something good somewhere, and she asks for money. I thought she was lonesome. She *said* she was.
THE GIRL	Maybe she was.
YOUNG MAN	She was *something*.
THE GIRL	I guess I'd never see you, if it didn't happen, though.
YOUNG MAN	Oh, I don't know—maybe I'd just mosey along this way and see you in this town somewhere. I'd recognize you, too.
THE GIRL	Recognize me?
YOUNG MAN	Sure, I'd recognize you the minute I laid eyes on you.
THE GIRL	Well, who would I be?
YOUNG MAN	Mine, that's who.
THE GIRL	Honest?
YOUNG MAN	Honest to God.
THE GIRL	You just say that because you're in jail.
YOUNG MAN	No, I mean it. You just pack up and wait for me. We'll high-roll the hell out of here to Frisco.
THE GIRL	You're just lonesome.
YOUNG MAN	I been lonesome all my life—there's no cure for that—but you and me—we can have a lot of fun hanging around together. You'll bring me luck. I know it.
THE GIRL	Why are you looking for luck for all the time?

YOUNG MAN   I'm a gambler. I don't work. I've *got* to have luck, or I'm a bum. I haven't had any decent luck in years. Two whole years now—one place to another. Bad luck all the time. That's why I got in trouble back there in Wheeling, too. That was no accident. That was my bad luck following me around. So here I am, with my head half busted. I guess it was her old man that did it.

THE GIRL   You mean her father?

YOUNG MAN   No, her husband. If I had an old lady like that, I'd throw her out.

THE GIRL   Do you think you'll have better luck, if I go with you?

YOUNG MAN   It's a cinch. I'm a good handicapper. All I need is somebody good like you with me. It's no good always walking around in the streets for anything that might be there at the time. You got to have somebody staying with you all the time— through winters when it's cold, and springtime when it's pretty, and summertime when it's nice and hot and you can go swimming—through *all* the times—rain and snow and all the different kinds of weather a man's got to go through before he dies. You got to have somebody who's right. Somebody who knows you, from away back. You got to have somebody who even knows you're wrong but likes you just the same. I know I'm wrong, but I just don't want anything the hard way, working like a dog, or the *easy* way, working like a dog—working's the hard way and the easy way both. All I got to do is beat the price, always—and then I don't feel lousy and don't hate anybody. If you go along with me, I'll be the finest guy anybody ever saw. I won't be wrong any more. You know when you get enough of

that money, you *can't* be wrong any more—
you're right because the money says so. I'll have
a lot of money and you'll be just about the pret-
tiest, most wonderful kid in the whole world.
I'll be proud walking around Frisco with you on
my arm and people turning around to look at us.

THE GIRL   Do you think they will?

YOUNG MAN   Sure they will. When I get back in some decent
clothes and you're on my arm—well, Katey,
they'll turn around and look, and they'll see something, too.

THE GIRL   Katey?

YOUNG MAN   Yeah—that's your name from now on. You're
the first girl I ever called Katey. I've been saving
it for you. O.K.?

THE GIRL   O.K.

YOUNG MAN   How long have I been here?

THE GIRL   Since last night. You didn't wake up until late
this morning, though.

YOUNG MAN   What time is it now? About nine?

THE GIRL   About ten.

YOUNG MAN   Have you got the key to this lousy cell?

THE GIRL   No. They don't let me fool with any keys.

YOUNG MAN   Well, can you get it?

THE GIRL   No.

YOUNG MAN   Can you *try?*

THE GIRL   They wouldn't let me get near any keys. I cook
for this jail, when they've got somebody in it. I
clean up and things like that.

YOUNG MAN   Well, I want to get out of here. Don't you know
the guy that runs this joint?

THE GIRL   I know him, but he wouldn't let you out. They
were talking of taking you to another jail in another town.

YOUNG MAN   Yeah? Why?

THE GIRL	Because they're afraid.
YOUNG MAN	What are they afraid of?
THE GIRL	They're afraid these people from Wheeling will come over in the middle of the night and break in.
YOUNG MAN	Yeah? What do they want to do that for?
THE GIRL	Don't *you* know what they want to do it for?
YOUNG MAN	Yeah, I know all right.
THE GIRL	Are you scared?
YOUNG MAN	Sure I'm scared. Nothing scares a man more than ignorance. You can argue with people who ain't fools, but you can't argue with fools—they just go to work and do what they're set on doing. Get me out of here.
THE GIRL	How?
YOUNG MAN	Well, go get the guy with the key, and let me talk to him.
THE GIRL	He's gone home. Everybody's gone home.
YOUNG MAN	You mean I'm in this little jail all alone?
THE GIRL	Well—yeah—except me.
YOUNG MAN	Well, what's the big idea—doesn't anybody stay here all the time?
THE GIRL	No, they go home every night. I clean up and then I go, too. I hung around tonight.
YOUNG MAN	What made you do that?
THE GIRL	I wanted to talk to you.
YOUNG MAN	Honest? What did you want to talk about?
THE GIRL	Oh, I don't know. I took care of you last night. You were talking in you sleep. You liked me, too. I didn't think you'd like me when you woke up, though.
YOUNG MAN	Yeah? Why not?
THE GIRL	I don't know.
YOUNG MAN	Yeah? Well, you're wonderful, see?
THE GIRL	Nobody ever talked to me that way. All the fellows in town—(*Pause*).

YOUNG MAN	What about 'em? Come on—tell me.
THE GIRL	They laugh at me.
YOUNG MAN	Laugh at you? They're fools. What do they know about anything? You go get your things and come back here. I'll take you with me to Frisco. How old are you?
THE GIRL	Oh, I'm of age.
YOUNG MAN	How old are you?—Don't lie to me! Sixteen?
THE GIRL	I'm seventeen.
YOUNG MAN	Well, bring your father and mother. We'll get married before we go.
THE GIRL	They wouldn't let me go.
YOUNG MAN	Why not?
THE GIRL	I don't know, but they wouldn't. I know they wouldn't.
YOUNG MAN	You go tell your father not to be a fool, see? What is he, a farmer?
THE GIRL	No—nothing. He gets a little relief from the government because he's supposed to be hurt or something—his side hurts, he says. I don't know what it is.
YOUNG MAN	Ah, he's a liar. Well, I'm taking you with me, see?
THE GIRL	He takes the money I earn, too.
YOUNG MAN	He's got no right to do that.
THE GIRL	I know it, but he does it.
YOUNG MAN	(almost to himself) This world stinks. You shouldn't have been born in this town, anyway, and you shouldn't have had a man like that for a father, either.
THE GIRL	Sometimes I feel sorry for him.
YOUNG MAN	Never mind feeling sorry for him. (Pointing a finger) I'm going to talk to your father some day. I've got a few things to tell that guy.
THE GIRL	I know you have.
YOUNG MAN	(suddenly) Hello—out there! See if you can get

	that fellow with the keys to come down and let me out.
THE GIRL	Oh, I couldn't.
YOUNG MAN	Why not?
THE GIRL	I'm nobody here—they give me fifty cents every day I work.
YOUNG MAN	How much?
THE GIRL	Fifty cents.
YOUNG MAN	(*to the world*) You see? They ought to pay money to *look* at you. To breathe the *air* you breathe. I don't know. Sometimes I figure it never is going to make sense. Hello—out there! I'm scared. You try to get me out of here. I'm scared them fools are going to come here from Wheeling and go crazy, thinking they're heroes. Get me out of here, Katey.
THE GIRL	I don't know what to do. Maybe I could break the door down.
YOUNG MAN	No, you couldn't do that. Is there a hammer out there or anything?
THE GIRL	Only a broom. Maybe they've locked the broom up, too.
YOUNG MAN	Go see if you can find anything.
THE GIRL	All right. (*She goes.*)
YOUNG MAN	Hello—out there! Hello—out there! (*Pause*) Hello—out there! Hello—out there! (*Pause*) Putting me in jail. (*With contempt*) Rape! Rape! *They* rape everything good that was ever born. His side hurts. They laugh at her. Fifty cents a day. Little punk people. Hurting the only good thing that ever came their way. (*Suddenly*) Hello —out there!
THE GIRL	(*returning*) There isn't a thing out there. They've locked everything up for the night.
YOUNG MAN	Any cigarettes?

THE GIRL	Everything's locked up—all the drawers of the desk, all the closet doors—everything.
YOUNG MAN	I ought to have a cigarette.
THE GIRL	I could get you a package maybe, somewhere. I guess the drug store's open. It's about a mile.
YOUNG MAN	A mile? I don't want to be alone that long.
THE GIRL	I could run all the way and all the way back.
YOUNG MAN	You're the sweetest girl that ever lived.
THE GIRL	What kind do you want?
YOUNG MAN	Oh, any kind—Chesterfields or Camels or Lucky Strikes—any kind at all.
THE GIRL	I'll go get a package. (*She turns to go.*)
YOUNG MAN	What about the money?
THE GIRL	I've got some money. I've got a quarter I been saving. I'll run all the way. (*She is about to go.*)
YOUNG MAN	Come here.
THE GIRL	(*going to him*) What?
YOUNG MAN	Give me your hand. (*He takes her hand and looks at it, smiling. He lifts it and kisses it.*) I'm scared to death.
THE GIRL	I am, too.
YOUNG MAN	I'm not lying—I don't care what happens to me, but I'm scared nobody will ever come out here to this God-forsaken broken-down town and find you. I'm scared you'll get used to it and not mind. I'm scared you'll get to Frisco and have 'em all turning around to look at you. Listen— go get me a gun, because if they come, I'll kill 'em! They don't understand. Get me a gun!
THE GIRL	I could get my father's gun. I know where he hides it.
YOUNG MAN	Go get it. Never mind the cigarettes. Run all the way. (*Pause, smiling but seriously*) Hello, Katey.
THE GIRL	Hello. What's *your* name?

YOUNG MAN	Photo-Finish is what they *call* me. My races are always photo-finish races. You don't know what that means, but it means they're very close. So close the only way they can tell which horse wins is to look at a photograph after the race is over. Well, every race I bet turns out to be a photo-finish race and my horse never wins. It's my bad luck, all the time. That's why they call me Photo-Finish. Say it before you go.
THE GIRL	Photo-Finish.
YOUNG MAN	Come here. (*The Girl moves close and he kisses her*) Now, hurry. Run all the way.
THE GIRL	I'll run. (*The Girl turns and runs. The Young Man stands at the center of the cell a long time. The Girl comes running back in. Almost crying*) I'm afraid. I'm afraid I won't see you again. If I come back and you're not here, I—
YOUNG MAN	Hello—out there!
THE GIRL	It's so lonely in this town. Nothing here but the lonesome wind all the time, lifting the dirt and blowing out to the prairie. I'll stay *here*. I won't *let* them take you away.
YOUNG MAN	Listen, Katey. Do what I tell you. Go get that gun and come back. Maybe they won't come tonight. Maybe they won't come at all. I'll hide the gun and when they let me out you can take it back and put it where you found it. And then we'll go away. But if they come, I'll kill 'em! Now, hurry—
THE GIRL	All right. (*Pause*) I want to tell you something.
YOUNG MAN	O.K.
THE GIRL	(*very softly*) If you're not here when I come back, well, I'll have the gun and I'll know what to do with it.
YOUNG MAN	You know how to handle a gun?

THE GIRL   I know how.

YOUNG MAN   Don't be a fool. (*Takes off his shoe, brings out some currency*) Don't be a fool, see? Here's some money. Eighty dollars. Take it and go to Frisco. Look around and find somebody. Find somebody alive and halfway human, see? Promise me—if I'm not here when you come back, just throw the gun away and get the hell to Frisco. Look around and find somebody.

THE GIRL   I don't *want* to find anybody.

YOUNG MAN   (*swiftly, desperately*) Listen, if I'm not here when you come back, how do you know I haven't gotten away? Now, do what I tell you. I'll meet you in Frisco. I've got a couple of dollars in my other shoe. I'll see you in San Francisco.

THE GIRL   (*with wonder*) San Francisco?

YOUNG MAN   That's right—San Francisco. That's where you and me belong.

THE GIRL   I've always wanted to go to *some* place like San Francisco—but how could I go alone?

YOUNG MAN   Well, you're not alone any more, see?

THE GIRL   Tell me a little what it's like.

YOUNG MAN   (*very swiftly, almost impatiently at first, but gradually slower and with remembrance, smiling, and the Girl moving closer to him as he speaks*) Well, it's on the Pacific to begin with—ocean water all around. Cool fog and seagulls. Ships from all over the world. It's got seven hills. The little streets go up and down, around and all over. Every night the fog-horns bawl. But they won't be bawling for you and me.

THE GIRL   What else?

YOUNG MAN   That's about all, I guess.

THE GIRL   Are people different in San Francisco?

YOUNG MAN   People are the same everywhere. They're different only when they love somebody. That's the only thing that makes 'em different. More people in Frisco love somebody, that's all.

THE GIRL   Nobody anywhere loves anybody as much as I love you.

YOUNG MAN   (*shouting, as if to the world*) You see? Hearing you say that, a man could die and still be ahead of the game. Now, hurry. And don't forget, if I'm not here when you come back, get the hell to San Francisco where you'll have a chance. Do you hear me? (*The Girl stands a moment looking at him, then backs away, turns and runs. The Young Man stares after her, troubled and smiling. Then he turns away from the image of her and walks about like a lion in a cage. After a while he sits down suddenly and buries his head in his hands. From a distance the sound of several automobiles approaching is heard. He listens a moment, then ignores the implications of the sound, whatever they may be. Several automobile doors are slammed. He ignores this also. A wooden door is opened with a key and closed, and footsteps are heard in a hall. Walking easily, almost casually and yet arrogantly, a Man comes in. The Young Man jumps up suddenly and shouts at the Man, almost scaring him*) What the hell kind of a jailkeeper are you, anyway? Why don't you attend to your business? You get paid for it, don't you? Now, get me out of here.

THE MAN   But I'm not the jailkeeper.

YOUNG MAN   Yeah? Well, who are you, then?

THE MAN   I'm the husband.

YOUNG MAN   What husband you talking about?

THE MAN   You know what husband.

YOUNG MAN   Hey! (*Pause, looking at the Man*) Are you the guy that hit me over the head last night?

THE MAN	I am.
YOUNG MAN	(*with righteous indignation*) What do you mean going around hitting people over the head?
THE MAN	Oh, I don't know. What do you mean going around—the way you do?
YOUNG MAN	(*rubbing his head*) You hurt my head. You got no right to hit anybody over the head.
THE MAN	(*suddenly angry, shouting*) Answer my question! What do you mean?
YOUNG MAN	Listen, you—don't be hollering at me just because I'm locked up.
THE MAN	(*with contempt, slowly*) You're a dog!
YOUNG MAN	Yeah, well, let me tell you something. You *think* you're the husband. You're the husband of nothing. (*Slowly*) What's more, your wife—if you want to call her that—is a tramp. Why don't you throw her out in the street where she belongs?
THE MAN	(*draws a pistol*) Shut up!
YOUNG MAN	Yeah? Go ahead, shoot—(*Softly*) and spoil the fun. What'll your pals think? They'll be disappointed, won't they? What's the fun hanging a man who's already dead? (*The Man puts the gun away*) That's right, because now you can have some fun yourself, telling me what you're going to do. That's what you came here for, isn't it? Well, you don't need to tell me. I *know* what you're going to do. I've read the papers and I know. They have fun. A mob of 'em fall on one man and beat him, don't they? They tear off his clothes and kick him, don't they? And women and little children stand around watching, don't they? Well, before you go on *this* picnic, I'm going to tell you a few things. Not that that's going to send you home with your pals—the other heroes. No. You've been outraged. A

stranger has come to town and violated your women. Your pure, innocent, virtuous women. You fellows have got to set this thing right. You're men, not mice. You're home-makers, and you beat your children. (*Suddenly*) Listen, you —I didn't know she was your wife. I didn't know she was anybody's wife.

THE MAN   You're a liar!

YOUNG MAN   Sometimes—when it'll do somebody some good —but not this time. Do you want to hear about it? (*The Man doesn't answer*) All right, I'll tell you. I met her at a lunch counter. She came in and sat next to me. There was plenty of room, but she sat next to me. Somebody had put a nickel in the phonograph and a fellow was singing *New San Antonio Rose*. Well, she got to talking about the song. I thought she was talking to the waiter, but *he* didn't answer her, so after a while *I* answered her. That's how I met her. I didn't think anything of it. We left the place together and started walking. The first thing I knew she said, This is where I live.

THE MAN   You're a dirty liar!

YOUNG MAN   Do you want to hear it? Or not? (*The Man does not answer*) O.K. She asked me to come in. Maybe she had something in mind, maybe she didn't. Didn't make any difference to me, one way or the other. If she was lonely, all right. If not, all right.

THE MAN   You're telling a lot of dirty lies!

YOUNG MAN   I'm telling the truth. Maybe your wife's out there with your pals. Well, call her in. I got nothing against her, or you—or any of you. Call her in, and ask her a few questions. Are you in love with her? (*The Man doesn't answer*) Well, that's too bad.

THE MAN	What do you mean, too bad?
YOUNG MAN	I mean this may not be the first time something like this has happened.
THE MAN	(*swiftly*) Shut up!
YOUNG MAN	Oh, you know it. You've always known it. You're afraid of your pals, that's all. She asked me for money. That's all she wanted. I wouldn't be here now if I had given her the money.
THE MAN	(*slowly*) How much did she ask for?
YOUNG MAN	I didn't ask her how much. I told her I'd made a mistake. She said she would make trouble if I didn't give her money. Well, I don't like bargaining, and I don't like being threatened, either. I told her to get the hell away from me. The next thing I knew she'd run out of the house and was hollering. (*Pause*) Now, why don't you go out there and tell 'em they took me to another jail—go home and pack up and leave her. You're a pretty good guy, you're just afraid of your pals. (*The Man draws his gun again. He is very frightened. He moves a step toward the Young Man, then fires three times. The Young Man falls to his knees. The Man turns and runs, horrified*) Hello—out there! (*He is bent forward. The Girl comes running in, and halts suddenly, looking at him.*)
THE GIRL	There were some people in the street, men and women and kids—so I came in through the back, through a window. I couldn't find the gun. I looked all over but I couldn't find it. What's the matter?
YOUNG MAN	Nothing—nothing. Everything's all right. Listen. Listen, kid. Get the hell out of here. Go out the same way you came in and run—run like hell—run all night. Get to another town and get on a train. Do you hear me?

THE GIRL	What's happened?
YOUNG MAN	Get away—just get away from here. Take any train that's going—you can get to Frisco later.
THE GIRL	(*almost sobbing*) I don't want to go any place without you.
YOUNG MAN	I can't go. Something's happened. (*He looks at her*) But I'll be with you always—God damn it. Always! (*He falls forward. The Girl stands near him, then begins to sob softly, walking away. She stands over to one side, stops sobbing, and stares out. The excitement of the mob outside increases. The Man, with two of his pals, comes running in. The Girl watches, unseen.*)
THE MAN	Here's the son of a bitch!
ANOTHER MAN	O.K. Open the cell, Harry.

(*The Third Man goes to the cell door, unlocks it, and swings it open.*) (*A Woman comes running in.*)

THE WOMAN	Where is he? I want to see him. Is he dead? (*Looking down at him, as the Men pick him up*) There he is. (*Pause*) Yeah, that's him. (*Her husband looks at her with contempt, then at the dead man.*)
THE MAN	(*trying to laugh*) All right—let's get it over with.
THIRD MAN	Right you are, George. Give me a hand, Harry. (*They lift the body.*)
THE GIRL	(*suddenly fiercely*) Put him down!
THE MAN	What's this?
SECOND MAN	What are you doing here? Why aren't you out in the street?
THE GIRL	Put him down and go away. (*She runs toward the men. The Woman grabs her.*)
THE WOMAN	Here—where do you think *you're* going?
THE GIRL	Let me go. You've no right to take him away.
THE WOMAN	Well, listen to her, will you? (*She slaps the Girl*

and pushes her to the floor) Listen to the little
slut, will you? (*They all go, carrying the Young
Man's body. The Girl gets up slowly, no longer
sobbing. She looks around, at everything, then
looks straight out, and whispers.*)

THE GIRL   Hello—out—there! Hello—out there!

Suggested interpretation

Unless a man or a woman is an accomplished impersonator
of the opposite sex, or unless this is given as a group or staged
reading, we have here a part dramatic and part nondramatic project
in interpretation. The reader may wish to *become* the character of
his own sex, but most likely he will merely *suggest* that of the
opposite sex. Suggesting (rather than becoming) a character, however, does not mean neglecting the task of interpretation.

Before discussing the interpretation let us consider the selection.
Hello Out There is very simple, there is no subtlety to the characterization, and the plot may even be unbelievable. Yet the play
almost unerringly penetrates to our innermost self. The very title
(so often repeated throughout the play) is symbolic of our most
pressing need—to communicate with a fellow human being, regardless of misfortune, of status, of education, or even of the
imminence of death. The play may be criticized by some for its
sentimentality and by others for its moral climate, but to be un-
moved by its humanity is nearly impossible.

The basic problem in interpretation is one of rhythm. There is
a contrasting tempo between the Young Man and the Girl that
reflects more than a difference in sex. It reflects background—the
restless transient life of the Young Man and the static, hopeless life
of the Girl; it also reflects temperament—the gambling instinct of
the Young Man and the domestic instinct of the Girl. In her he
finds a sure bet, in him she finds a protector and a mate.

Reading the two parts will require as much attention to the
person of the opposite sex as to the person of one's own sex. The
problem is analogous to that of counterpoint in music. One must
master two separate and equally important melodies; the harmony
is the product of both melodies.

For the male, the problem becomes one of adjusting to the
relatively weaker, slower, less impetuous, but equally impassioned

tones of the Girl. For the female, the problem is that of adjusting to the stronger, more impetuous, and less rational vocal patterns of the Young Man. Technically, it is necessary to make a contrast in body tension and a less but still noticeable contrast in pitch level between the characters. The contrast must be consistent, however.

The rapidity of the dialogue probably will make difficult any shift in position of the feet or even of the head in reading each part. If you do manage to shift your eyes each time, consider that the Young Man will look downwards, and the Girl will look upwards—a customary method for making a distinction between the sexes.

There is little straight narrative other than the initial stage directions and those at the end where the husband, the wife, and the mob enter. Such directions probably should be read directly to the audience.

As for details, the most perplexing phrase to interpret is the theme: "Hello out there." Should the Young Man say the line as if he expects an answer? Should he say it the same way each time? Obviously, when he hears the Girl answer him he calls to her directly, but how about the other times? And then, at the last line of the play will the Girl attempt to imitate the Young Man or will she reflect her own newly found self?

Be cautious in reading the Young Man's lines. It is important that they be philosophical rather than sentimental. You may have similar difficulty in reading his description of San Francisco. Be careful, too, that you do not strike a false note in reading the Girl's affirmation of love.

When the Man comes in, after he is identified and the Young Man asks him why he goes around "hitting people over the head," he replies almost out of character, "Oh, I don't know. What do you mean going around—the way you do?" How is this line to be interpreted? Is the first sentence sarcastic and the second belligerent? Is the first reflective and the second suspicious? Is either "you" given a strong stress?

It is not too important whether or not the newcomers at the end of the scene are given specific characterizations so long as it is clear what they say and do. The story is really finished before they come in.

VI

PRESENTATION OF VERSE MATERIAL

We are the music makers,
And we are the dreamers of dreams,
Wandering by lone sea-breakers,
And sitting by desolate streams;
World-losers and world-forsakers,
On whom the pale moon gleams:
Yet we are the movers and shakers
Of the world for ever, it seems.

With wonderful deathless ditties
We build up the world's great cities,
And out of a fabulous story
We fashion an empire's glory:
One man with a dream, at pleasure,
Shall go forth and conquer a crown;
And three with a new song's measure
Can trample an empire down.

We, in the ages lying
In the buried past of the earth,
Built Nineveh with our sighing,
And Babel itself with our mirth;
And o'erthrew them with prophesying
To the old of the new world's worth;
For each age is a dream that is dying,
Or one that is coming to birth.

(ARTHUR O'SHAUGHNESSY, *Ode*)

Poetry is read for pleasure. It appeals to the imagination. Feeling and mood are of major importance. They are the windows through which we look to see imagery, fantasy, and beauty. To realize this pleasure for himself and for us, the poet expresses himself in a form more rigid and exacting than is usually found in prose. The differences between poetry and prose may only be differences of degree, but they are such that special attention must be paid to them in oral reading. This is particularly true for the proper handling of rhythm and metrical form. The factors of voice described in Chapter II must be employed differently, especially those of stress and pause.

Poetry is written for the ear. We get the most enjoyment from it when we can hear the rhythms. To interpret the rhythms one should understand them. The study need not be as intensive as it would be if you were to write poetry, but it should be sufficiently thorough for you to do justice to your interpretation. Probably the main reason poetry is often read so poorly is that the reader does not recognize the rhythmic movement. Either the reading is nothing but sing-song, or the rhythm is so violated that the reading jolts along brokenly and unintelligently. There must be a happy harmony between the rhythm of a poem, on the one hand, and the sense stress and thought groupings, on the other.

1   CHARACTERISTICS OF VERSE

a   Rhythm and meter

We define *rhythm* as a more or less regular recurrence of a recognizable pattern, and it is found in any art form. In all good writing, but especially in poetry, the pattern is discovered in word structure. In conventional verse, rhythm is the perceptible alternation of accented and unaccented syllables in the flow of words. This alternation can be measured—in metrical terms. *Meter* is the arrangement and number of accented and unaccented syllables that fall within each line. In free verse the pattern cannot be so measured, but it still can be discovered. We shall concern ourselves first with the rhythms of metered verse.

b   Metrical accent

In Chapter II we described the relation between natural accent and sense stress. Now we introduce *metrical accent,* the noticeable beat that occurs with relative regularity. Ordinarily, metrical accent coincides with natural accent; it also can fall on words of one syllable. Sense stress falls only on the idea-carrying words (whether these have one or more than one syllable) but nowhere else. So there are many syllables that receive metrical accent and no sense stress, and, not infrequently, some syllables receive sense stress where there is no metrical accent.

The problem that immediately concerns us in reading metered poetry aloud is this: how much should we adhere to the metrical accent? Should we follow it uniformly or should we vary it? What should we do when sense stress appears where there is no metrical accent? And what should we do with metrical accents where there is no sense stress?

Some poems lend themselves to a rather pronounced "sounding out" of the metrical accent. In others the metrical accent should be played down. In still others there should be a harmonious compromise. It is only after an adequate consideration of the metrical pattern, the type of poetry, the thought and feeling content, and the mood and intent of the author that a decision can be made. There are certain general suggestions, however, that may be given.

Mother Goose rhymes (and light humorous verse) seem to call for a rather strict adherence to the metrical beat.* Certainly children insist on it.

> Híckory, díckory, dóck
> The moúse ran úp the clóck
> The clóck struck óne; the moúse ran dówn
> Híckory, díckory, dóck.

> Óld Mother Húbbard, wént to the cúpboard
> To gét her poor dóg a bóne
> But whén she got thére, the cúpboard was báre
> And só the poor dóg had nóne.

---

* Here, accent marks will be placed above the syllables receiving the metrical accent.

Jáck be nímble,

Jáck be quíck

Jáck jump óver the cándlestíck.

Lear, Gilbert, and some of Ogden Nash should be read with free
rein given to the metrical beat. (Refer to "The Jumblies," "The
Owl and the Pussy Cat," and "The Modern Major-General," in
Chapter II.)

In narrative poetry (including ballads), although we should
read with moderate shifts of tempo, duration, and feeling tones in
order to avoid a sing-song effect, the metrical accent can be
judiciously preserved; indeed it enhances the charm. Sense stress
and metrical accent usually coincide.

You may tálk of gin and beér

When you're quártered safe out 'ére,

And you're sént to penny fíghts and Aldershót it;

But whén it comes to sláughter

You will dó your work on wáter,

And you'll líck the bloomin' boóts of 'im that's gót it.

(KIPLING, *Gunga Din*)

I clósed my líds and képt them clósed,

And the bálls like púlses beát;

For the ský and the seá, and the seá and the ský

Láy like a loád on my weáry éye,

And the deád were át my feét.

(COLERIDGE, *The Rime of the Ancient Mariner*)

Metrical accent may need to be modified and subordinated,
however, in reading more reflective and lyrical poetry. Here, we
shall underline the accented syllables of the idea-carrying words

to show more clearly the relation between sense stress and metrical accent. Where the two marks coincide, the metrical accent should be heavier than it is elsewhere. Where accent marks are placed in parentheses, the metrical accent should be softened or omitted.

> Hail to thee, blithe Spirit!
> Bird thou never wert,
> That from Heaven, or near it
> Pourest thy full heart
> In profuse strains of unpremeditated art.

> (SHELLEY, *To a Skylark*)

> Tomorrow, and tomorrow, and tomorrow,
> Creeps in this petty pace from day to day
> To the last syllable of recorded time.
> And all our yesterdays have lighted fools
> The way to dusty death. Out, out, brief candle
> Life's but a walking shadow, a poor player
> That struts and frets his hour upon the stage
> And then is heard no more: it is a tale
> Told by an idiot, full of sound and fury,
> Signifying nothing.

> (*Macbeth*, V, 5)

c Metrical forms

Merely to be aware of metrical accent is not enough. Unless we are also familiar with the principal metrical forms we may not be able to discover the accents at all, or, what is worse, we may pick up the wrong ones. You must master the meter or the meter will master you!

A line of poetry is called a *verse* (not to be confused with the *stanza* which is a larger unit of the poem consisting of several verses). The traditional unit of the verse is called the *foot*. The foot establishes the metrical pattern of the poem. It gives us the particular combination of accented and unaccented syllables that are rather consistently repeated in the verse. There must be at least one accented syllable in each foot.

The commonest metrical foot used in poetry is the *iambic* foot. In a general way it follows the basic rhythm of all Germanic languages. It consists of one unaccented followed by one accented syllable.

> The Curfew tolls the knell of parting day,
>   The lowing herd winds slowly o'er the lea,
> The plowman homeward plods his weary way,
>   And leaves the world to darkness and to me.
>
>   (GRAY, *Elegy written in a Country Churchyard*)

Just the reverse of this, an accented followed by an unaccented syllable, is the *trochaic* foot.

> Ah, distinctly I remember it was in the bleak December;
> And each separate dying ember wrought its ghost upon the floor.
>
>   (POE, *The Raven*)

A succession of two unaccented followed by one accented syllable is called the *anapaestic* foot.

> For the moon never beams without bringing me dreams
>   Of the beautiful Annabel Lee;
>
>   (POE, *Annabel Lee*)

The reverse of this, one long syllable followed by two short, is a *dactyllic* foot.

One more Unfortunate,   8
Weary of breath,
Rashly importunate,
Gone to her death!

(HOOD, *The Bridge of Sighs*)

Another form not so well known but very enjoyable is the dipodic foot—a combination of two trochaic or two iambic feet in such a way that they become one long and three short beats or three short and one long. Kipling's "Gunga Din," already quoted, is an example. His "Mandalay" is another (only two unaccented beats occur in the first foot).

By the old Moulmein Pagoda, lookin' eastward to the sea,
There's a Burma girl a settin', and I know she thinks of me.

Note: It will not be necessary for the needs of the oral reader to describe other less frequently used feet. Spondees and pyrrhics, for instance, are primarily visual rather than audible forms.

The metrical form of the poem gets its name not only from the kind of foot used but also from the number of feet in each verse. Thus:

iambic dimeter (two feet)   iambic hexameter (six feet)
iambic trimeter (three feet)   iambic septameter (seven feet)
iambic tetrameter (four feet)   iambic octameter (eight feet)
iambic pentameter (five feet)

The same combinations are possible with trochaic, anapaestic, dactylic, and dipodic feet. (Note the length of the verses quoted in this section and in the next.)

Occasionally, one will come across some unusual form which still has a very marked rhythm. William Rose Benét's "Jesse James," and Vachel Lindsay's "The Congo" are examples.

In "Jesse James" a strong four-beat line predominates except in the parenthetical expressions which have two beats. But there is such variation in the composition of the individual feet that any traditional classification would be of small value. In addition to the strength of the beat there is an impelling tempo that cannot be ignored. The tempo is halved within the parentheses which equalizes the halving of the beats. Then, in the stanzas where there are no parentheses, the over-all tempo is more rapid than in those stanzas containing them. Try reading it and see if you don't observe these characteristics.

Jesse James *

BY WILLIAM ROSE BENÉT

Jesse James was a two-gun man,
　　(*Roll on, Missouri!*)
Strong-arm chief of an outlaw clan.
　　(*From Kansas to Illinois!*)
He twirled an old Colt forty-five;
　　(*Roll on, Missouri!*)
They never took Jesse James alive.
　　(*Roll, Missouri, roll!*)

Jesse James was King of the Wes';
　　(*Cataracts in the Missouri!*)
He'd a di'mon' heart in his lef' breas';
　　(*Brown Missouri rolls!*)
He'd a fire in his heart no hurt could stifle;
　　(*Thunder, Missouri!*)
Lion eyes an' a Winchester rifle.
　　(*Missouri, roll down!*)

Jesse James rode a pinto hawse;
Come at night to a water-cawse;
Tetched with the rowel that pinto's flank;
She sprung the torrent from bank to bank.

* Reprinted by permission of Dodd, Mead & Company from *Golden Fleece* by William Rose Benét. Copyright 1933, 1935 by Dodd, Mead & Company, Inc.

Jesse rode through a sleepin' town;
Looked the moonlit street both up an' down;
Crack-crack-crack, the street ran flames
An' a great voice cried, "I'm Jesse James!"

Hawse an' afoot they're after Jess!
    (*Roll on, Missouri!*)
Spurrin' an' spurrin'—but he's gone Wes';
    (*Brown Missouri rolls!*)
He was ten foot tall when he stood in his boots;
    (*Lightnin' like the Missouri!*)
More'n a match fer sich galoots.
    (*Roll, Missouri, roll!*)

Jesse James rode outa the sage;
Roun' the rocks come the swayin' stage;
Straddlin' the road a giant stan's
An' a great voice bellers, "Throw up yer han's!"

Jesse raked in the di'mon' rings,
The big gold watches an' the yuther things;
Jesse divvied 'em then an' thar
With a cryin' child had lost her mar.

They're creepin'; they're crawlin'; they're stalkin' Jess;
    (*Roll on Missouri!*)
They's a rumor he's gone much further Wes';
    (*Roll, Missouri, roll!*)
They's word of a cayuse hitched to the bars
    (*Ruddy clouds on Missouri!*)
Of a golden sunset that busts into stars.
    (*Missouri, roll down!*)

Jesse James rode hell fer leather;
He was a hawse an' a man together;
In a cave in a mountain high up in air
He lived with a rattlesnake, a wolf, an' a bear.

Jesse's heart was as sof' as a woman;
Fer guts an' stren'th he was sooper-human;
He could put six shots through a woodpecker's eye
And take in one swaller a gallon o' rye.

They sought him here an' they sought him there,
    (*Roll on, Missouri!*)
But he strides by night through the ways of the air;
    (*Brown Missouri, rolls!*)
They say he was took an' they say he is dead,
    (*Thunder, Missouri!*)
But he ain't—he's a sunset overhead!
    (*Missouri down to the sea!*)

Jesse James was a Hercules,
When he went through the woods he tore up the trees.
When he went on the plains he smoked the groun'
An' the hull lan' shuddered fer miles aroun'.

Jesse James wore a red bandanner
That waved on the breeze like the Star Spangled Banner;
In seven states he cut up dadoes.
He's gone with the buffer an' the desperadoes.

Yes, Jesse James was a two-gun man
    (*Roll on, Missouri!*)
The same as when this song began;
    (*From Kansas to Illinois!*)
An' when you see a sunset bust into flames
    (*Lightnin' like the Missouri!*)
Or a thunderstorm blaze—that's Jesse James!
    (*Hear that Missouri roll!*)

In "The Congo," familiar to all, there is likewise a four-beat
line or combinations of two-beat lines that run together when
read aloud. Here, too, the individual feet are varied in composition.
There are marked variations in tempo within the line as well as

between sections of the poem. Yet, through it all comes the steady rhythm suggestive of the tom-tom of the Congo or the drum of the revival meeting.

d   Variations of metrical forms

We have noticed that in some poems the metrical accent can be given more prominence than in others, but in most of our poetry a degree of variety is called for. Such variation may be discovered in the very structure of the poem itself, and now that we are acquainted with the basic metrical forms it is possible to recognize the variations and make use of this knowledge in our oral reading.

(1) Observe where one or more metrical forms is substituted for the prevailing one.

> It is an ancient Mariner
>
> And he stoppeth one of three.

(COLERIDGE, *The Rime of the Ancient Mariner*)

Here, in the second verse, the first foot is anapaestic. The rest are all iambic.

Once upon a midnight dreary, while I pondered weak and weary,
Over many a quaint and curious volume of forgotten lore—

(POE, *The Raven*)

Here, in the second verse, the second foot is dactylic, the fourth foot could be dactylic, while the rest are all trochaic.

(2) Watch for places where unaccented syllables are either added to or dropped from a foot. This often occurs at the beginning and end of a verse.

> We are the music makers,
>
> And we are the dreamers of dreams,
>
> Wandering by lone sea breakers,
>
> And sitting by desolate streams

(ARTHUR O'SHAUGHNESSY, *Ode*)

Here, the prevailing meter is dactylic. An unaccented syllable is
added at the beginning of the second and fourth verses. One is
dropped at the end of the first and third verses. Notice that these
two variations equalize each other. Notice also that the second
foot in both the first and third verses is a trochaic substitution.
In the last foot of the second and fourth verses both unaccented
syllables are dropped. A compensating pause is possible here.

> She will start from her slumber
> When gusts shake the door,
> She will hear the winds howling,
> Will hear the waves roar.

> (MATTHEW ARNOLD, *The Forsaken Merman*)

Here, the prevailing meter is anapaestic. An unaccented syllable
is added at the end of the first and third verse and one is dropped
from the beginning of the second and fourth verses. This last can
also be considered a case of substitution of an iambic for an
anapaestic foot.

(3) Watch for "run-on" lines. This is but an application of the
technique of pausing between thought groups. The problem pe-
culiar to poetry is that the verse does not necessarily correspond
to a sentence or even to a thought group; but, because the verse
is a complete unit in itself, one naturally tends to pause at the
end. We must note each line to see whether a pause is justified
there or not. It is often advisable to pause within the verse as the
sense dictates. Such a pause is called a *caesura*.

> She walks in beauty, like the night
> Of cloudless climes and starry skies;
> And all that's best of dark and bright
> Meet in her aspect and her eyes:

> (BYRON, *She Walks in Beauty*)

Here, the meaning would be lost completely if you pause after
"night." The verse cuts the thought group in two. You might pause
momentarily, though, after "bright." The latter illustrates the pos-

sibility of a natural pause between subject and predicate—where no punctuation marks exist.

> The waves beside them danced, but they
> Out-did the sparkling waves in glee:
> A poet could not but be gay,
> In such a jocund company:
>
> (WORDSWORTH, *Daffodils*)

Here, obviously, there should be no pause at the end of the first verse.

(4) Notice the rhyme scheme and avoid making it too prominent. When succeeding or alternating verses rhyme, as they do in so many poems, there is a tendency for the reader to make too much of it. Once one member of the pair is sounded, the reader often forgets all else until he sounds the other member. The second sound draws like a magnet.

This fault is often linked with the failure to make run-on lines. When, in addition to this, the reader makes the metrical accent too prominent, you have the perfect example of poetry read at its worst! The reader has completely succumbed to the lilt and reads without meaning.

There are variations in this following excerpt from Wolsey's famous farewell speech to Cromwell (*Henry VIII,* iii. 2), variations in tempo and intensity as well as in metrical form. Can you find them?

> And when I am forgotten, as I shall be,
> And sleep in dull cold marble, where no mention
> Of me more must be heard of, say, I taught thee,
> Say, Wolsey, that once trod the ways of glory,
> And sounded all the depths and shoals of honour,
> Found thee a way, out of his wreck, to rise in;
> A sure and safe one, though thy master miss'd it.
> Mark but my fall, and that that ruin'd me.
> Cromwell, I charge thee, fling away ambition:
> By that sin fell the angels; how can man then,
> The image of his Maker, hope to win by 't?

e   Non-metrical rhythms

One large area of poetry cannot be described at all in the metrical terms we have been using. This is the area of *free verse* (not to be confused with blank verse, which will be defined later), in which so much modern poetry has been written. It has form, definitely, but the form defies classification. Verses (lines of poetry) are separated from each other—each usually beginning with a capital letter—but they contain neither a predominant type of metered foot nor the same number of feet per verse. Instead of a regular recurrence of accented and unaccented syllables we find a recurrence of identical words, of similar sentence structure, or an alternation of long and short lines. We even notice a recurrence of rhyme schemes. Not infrequently the rhythmic pattern of free verse is a visual one—the arrangement of words on a page—like a pictorial design. In this last case it is extremely difficult to design a vocal pattern of interpretation that will match the visual one on the printed page.

Let there be no mistake. Good free verse is not careless verse. A sense of discipline is as important in the writing (and in the reading) as it is in the most rigid of conventional forms. Free verse, however, does permit more variety, more experimentation, and a wider use of imagination.

Walt Whitman, an early pioneer in this field, has been followed by so many worthwhile poets that it is impossible to select names except at random. John Gould Fletcher, Stephen Vincent Benét, Edgar Lee Masters, Robinson Jeffers, Dylan Thomas, Carl Sandburg, E. E. Cummings, Conrad Aiken, Kenneth Fearing, Marianne Moore, and a host of others could be included.

Let us illustrate free verse with "The Hollow Men" by T. S. Eliot.* In Part V, for instance, there is the travesty nursery rhyme in the beginning followed by three divisions, each beginning with the same word sequence and each ending with a refrain. But the third division is two lines longer than the other two, and the second refrain is different from the first and third. Then the first words of each refrain are set down in order. There is variety throughout this part of the poem. But then the final lines:

* From *Collected Poems* 1909-1935 by T. S. Eliot, copyright 1936 by Harcourt, Brace & World, Inc., and reprinted with their permission and permission of Faber and Faber, Ltd., London.

> This is the way the world ends
> This is the way the world ends
> This is the way the world ends
> Not with a bang but a whimper.

exemplify extreme regularity.

In Eliot's "Portrait of a Lady" * we have unexpected irregular recurrences of rhyme:

> And four wax candles in the darkened room,
> Four rings of light upon the ceiling overhead,
> An atmosphere of Juliet's tomb

and

> Now that lilacs are in bloom
> She has a bowl of lilacs in her room

Then there is the constant recurrence of the theme line:

> I shall sit here, serving tea to friends.

Amy Lowell's "Patterns" † is in itself a fascinating rhythmic pattern. Here we have an alternation between the repression of the present: the staccato lines describing the rigid movements of the protagonist as she faces the reality of her lover's death, and the abandon of yesterday: the relaxed liquid sounds of the lines that reveal her recollections of the time they were together. In the same poem we also have unexpected rhymes:

> And all the daffodils
> Are blowing, and the bright blue squills.
> The daffodils and squills

* From *Collected Poems* 1909-1935 by T. S. Eliot, copyright 1936 by Harcourt, Brace & World, Inc., and reprinted with their permission and permission of Faber and Faber, Ltd., London.
† From *The Complete Works of Amy Lowell.* Reprinted by permission of Houghton Mifflin Company.

Flutter in the breeze
As they please.
And I weep;
For the lime tree is in blossom
And one small flower has dropped upon my bosom.

The rhythms of free verse, so different from those of conventional verse, can be very satisfying even though they may be elusive. They will be most satisfying when you can weave all of the factors of voice into a pattern of interpretation that will reflect them. Let the nature of the rhythm be your guide. Where there is uniformity let your voice reproduce the uniformity, and where there is variety, let your voice reproduce the variety. Avoid monotony, avoid affectation, but do not ignore the possibilities for re-creating the art of the poet whom you interpret.

f Types of poetry

It is helpful to know not only the basic rhythmic forms, but also a few basic types of poetry which employ certain of these forms rather consistently. If you recognize the type, you will be alerted to the problems of oral interpretation that are related to it.

The sonnet is probably the most rigid metrical form, for the structure is pre-established, although even here, variations do occur. In general, the sonnet consists of fourteen lines of iambic pentameter. There are two major types, however. The *Italian sonnet* (Petrarchan) contains an octave (eight lines) with the rhyme scheme, *a b b a a b b a,* and a sestet (six lines) with the rhyme scheme, *c d e c d e,* or some variation of this. When the poet uses this form he usually divides his thought into two parts. In the octave he develops a general problem or theme, and in the sestet he resolves the problem or speculates upon the theme. Or a generalization is asserted in the octave and a particular application is made in the sestet. The two sonnets by Keats and Wordsworth (see Chapter IV) were written in the form of the Italian sonnet.

The *English sonnet* (or Shakespearian sonnet) consists of three quatrains and a couplet. The rhyme scheme is *a b a b c d c d e f-e f g g.* When the poet employs this form he usually states a general theme in the first quatrain, develops one aspect of it in the second, another in the third, and then makes an epigrammatic comment in the couplet. A variation, or actually a combination of the two types, is the *Spenserian sonnet, a b a b b c b c c d c d e e,* which permits greater integration of the three quatrains.

> One day I wrote her name upon the strand,
> But came the waves and washed it away:
> Again I wrote it with a second hand,
> But came the tide, and made my pains his prey.
> Vain man, said she, that dost in vain assay
> A mortal thing so to immortalize!
> For I myself shall like to this decay,
> And eek my name be wipèd out likewise.
> Not so (quoth I) let baser things devise
> To die in dust, but you shall live by fame:
> My verse your virtues rare shall eternize,
> And in the heavens write your glorious name.
> Where, whenas death shall all the world subdue
> Our love shall live and later life renew.
>
> (SPENSER, *Amoretti*)

When you recognize the type of sonnet (noting the rhyme scheme is the easiest way) you can usually discover how the thought is developed. Then you can select a pattern of interpretation that will reveal this thought development.

The structure of the ballad is also pre-established. Its most common form is a four-line stanza of alternating iambic tetrameter and iambic trimeter lines rhyming *a b c b,* but here, too, there are variations. Sometimes the meter is anapaestic (as in "Lord Randal," pp. 136-7); sometimes the ballad consists of couplets; sometimes there are six lines to the stanza; and frequently a refrain is added. The ballad tells a simple story and the thought development is quite uniform.

There are two general types of ballads, each of which calls for a difference in interpretation. The *folk ballad,* probably composed as a group project with the aid of a minstrel (or his modern equivalent) spins a yarn. The yarn is objective, boldly told, and uncomplicated.

Sir Patrick Spence

The King sits in Dumferling toune,
Drinking the blude-reid wine:
"O whare will I get guid sailor,
To sail this schip of mine?"

Up and spak an eldern knicht,
Sat at the King's richt kne:
"Sir Patrick Spence is the best sailor
That sails upon the se."

The King had written a braid letter,
And signd it wi his hand,
And sent it to Sir Patrick Spence,
Was walking on the sand.

The first line that Sir Patrick red,
A loud lauch lauched he;
The next line that Sir Patrick red,
The teir blinded his ee.

"O wha is this has don this deid,
This ill deid done to me,
To send me out this time o' the yeir,
To sail upon the se?

"Mak haste, mak haste, my mirry men all,
Our guid schip sails the morne."
"O say na sae, my master deir,
For I feir a deadlie storme.

"Late late yestreen I saw the new moone,
Wi the auld moone in her arme,
And I feir, I feir, my deir master,
That we will cum to harme."

O our Scots nobles wei richt laith
To weet thair cork-heild schoone;
Bot lang owre a' the play wer playd,
Thair hats they swam aboone.

O lang, lang may thair ladies sit,
Wi thair fans into thair hand;
Or eir they se Sir Patrick Spence
Cum sailing to the land.

O lang, lang may the ladies stand,
Wi thair gold kems in thair hair,
Waiting for thair ain deir lords,
For they'll se thame na mair.

Haf owre, haf owre to Aberdour,
It's fiftie fadom deip,
And thair lies guid Sir Patrick Spence,
Wi the Scots lords at his feit.

The progression of a folk ballad usually follows a time sequence. When you read to others you should pattern your interpretation accordingly. This means a straight, warm, objective reading devoid of vocal pyrotechnics and certainly of physical maneuvers.

The *literary ballad* is written by an individual poet. (We have quoted from Coleridge's *The Rime of the Ancient Mariner,* a literary ballad, elsewhere in this text.) Here you will find that the author tends to moralize as he tells the tale. Insofar as his own sentiments are introduced, a subjective factor is added. (When such sentiment becomes sentimental the ballad had best be discarded!) Your interpretation should most likely reveal these sentiments superimposed, as it were, upon the unfolding story.

The structure of other metrical forms is not so easily marked, except in such special types as the *ballade,* a French form having three stanzas with a rigid rhyme scheme, and an envoy. You might discover the three movements of the classic *Pindaric ode,* but this is a rare form. *Blank verse,* unrhymed iambic pentameter, developed by the Elizabethans (including Shakespeare) and used successfully since then by such poets as Browning (*The Ring and the Book*), Matthew Arnold (*Sohrab and Rustum*), and in this

century by Maxwell Anderson, Robinson Jeffers, Edwin Arlington
Robinson, and others, must be analyzed like narrative prose without the benefit of paragraphing. Some *lyrics* are written in stanzaic
form and some are not. The thought development must be discovered in each of them separately.

In *free verse* you may find the thought development corresponds
to some unusual spatial structure on the printed page such as may
be found in T. S. Eliot or E. E. Cummings. Or it may lie in the
ridiculous spelling rhymes that often delight us in reading Ogden
Nash. Take care when you translate the humor of the spelling
into sound! The numerical notations in Hanniel Long's "Students"
or Wallace Stevens's "Thirteen Ways of Looking at a Blackbird"
give us the key to their structure.

Whether you will prefer to read poetry composed in the more
conventional metrical patterns, or whether you will find more
satisfaction in verse freed from the metered beat, or whether,
more happily, you will find pleasure in both the old and the new,
as is often the case with the lover of music, you will probably be
guided as much by your sensitivity to rhythmic patterns as by
your interest in the subject matter. A rhythmic sense must be
cultivated. Do not eschew the classic form, such as the sonnet,
for there is no challenge greater to the poet or to his oral interpreter than that of compressing the most magnificent of sentiments
in the most exacting of frameworks. Do not treat the moderns
with contempt, either. The poet whose mind and heart are disciplined may reach great heights through a medium freed from
conventional rules, providing his sense of rhythm is not dulled.
You will enjoy reading poetry aloud, the subject matter of which
you can appreciate and the rhythmic pattern to which you can
attune.

2   STUDIES IN READING POETRY

a   A ballad

Lord Randal

"O where hae ye been, Lord Randal, my son?
O where hae ye been, my handsome young man?"—
"I hae been to the wild wood; mother, make my bed soon,
For I'm weary wi' hunting, and fain wald lie down."

"Where gat ye your dinner, Lord Randal, my son?
Where gat ye your dinner, my handsome young man?"—
"I din'd wi' my true-love; mother, make my bed soon,
For I'm weary wi' hunting, and fain wald lie down."

"What gat ye to your dinner, Lord Randal, my son?
What gat ye to your dinner, my handsome young man?"—
"I gat eels boiled in broo'; mother, make my bed soon,
For I'm weary wi' hunting, and fain wald lie down."

"What became of your bloodhounds, Lord Randal, my son?
What became of your bloodhounds, my handsome young man?"—
"O they swell'd and they died; mother, make my bed soon,
For I'm weary wi' hunting, and fain wald lie down."

"O I fear ye are poison'd, Lord Randal, my son!
O I fear ye are poison'd, my handsome young man!"—
"O yes! I am poison'd; mother, make my bed soon,
For I'm sick at the heart and I fain wald lie down."

Suggested interpretation

The old English ballad tells a story; it neither moralizes nor sentimentalizes. Its structure is simple, its unfolding plot is simple, its telling is simple. Its worth lies in the accuracy with which a basic trait of human nature is caught (here, the tendency to enter into an amorous relation too hastily), in the economy of words used, and in the impact on the imagination which can stir up myriad associations for reflection.

Lord Randal has all of these things. It must be inferred that some tragic flaw in the hero's nature or that of his "true-love" led inevitably to the fatal poisoning. That he came home to die, that his mother had the stamina to get to the bottom of the case, that there is no need to speculate as to possible revenge—all seem fitting.

The basic interpretation *must* be simple, restrained, regular. This involves a minimum of variation in pitch, tempo, intensity, and even quality. The fact that this ballad has been read on the air and public platform with such anguish of soul and tear-jerking sentiment indicates that far too many prefer pyrotechnics to artistry.

Insofar as a proper rhyme scheme is one of the details of interpretation you must be acquainted with the Middle English pronunciations in the poem. The rhyme scheme is *a a b b,* "man" rhymes with "son" and "down" with "soon."

Anapaestic tetrameter predominates, but there are a sufficient number of substitutions to permit a break in the extreme regularity of the basic meter. For instance, a break is permitted in the middle of the first two verses in each stanza because of the iambic substitution. Then in the third verse there is a dipodic substitution:

"I hae béen/to the wíld/wood; mother, máke/my bed sóon," which suggests a slight stumble (a caesura) as if the attention of Lord Randal cannot long be held on the answer he is giving but rushes back to his basic need for mother, bed, and death.

Metrical accent and sense stress coincide fairly well throughout, but wouldn't you stress "am" rather than "poison'd" in the third verse of the last stanza? The concept has been made clear already. This is the final admission. Would a pause for effect here enhance the mood?

Work out a detailed interpretation to embrace these suggestions and your own ideas. They must be fairly definite or you will distort the unity and mar the simplicity. This is truly a fine poem. Keep it so by reading with restraint. There is music enough in the rhythm and pathos enough in the story. You need not add any of your own.

b   A sonnet

Euclid alone has looked on Beauty bare *

BY EDNA ST. VINCENT MILLAY

Euclid alone has looked on Beauty bare.
Let all who prate of Beauty hold their peace,
And lay them prone upon the earth and cease
To ponder on themselves, the while they stare
At nothing, intricately drawn nowhere

In shapes of shifting lineage; let geese
Gabble and hiss, but heroes seek release
From dusty bondage into luminous air.
O blinding hour, O holy, terrible day,
When first the shaft into his vision shone
Of light anatomized! Euclid alone
Has looked on Beauty bare. Fortunate they
Who, though once only and then but far away,
Have heard her massive sandal set on stone.

Suggested interpretation

A perfect form for the praise of pure form. The subject matter of this sonnet is pure abstraction, but the "blinding hour" of insight made an emotional impact on Euclid of considerable magnitude. What emotional effect is made on you? What emotional effect might you seek to produce for your audience?

Notice the progression of parts, corresponding approximately to that of the Italian sonnet. The octave consists of three thoughts: the thesis (line 1), the advice to lovers of Beauty (lines 2-6), and the analogy (lines 6-8). Then, in the sestet, there is a quatrain in which is revealed the intensity of the vision, ending with the repetition of the thesis. The last two lines suggest the possibility that others may share this rare experience. Keep these thoughts separate, one from the other, in your reading. Take care here, for several times the thought begins within the line rather than at its beginning. The climax, of course, is at the vision. Your decision regarding the emotional content of the sonnet will govern your method of interpreting this climax.

Let us comment on two detailed problems of interpretation. Notice how the poet suggests the need for a silent contemplation of the infinite, as a prerequisite for gaining insight into mathematical beauty, by using a preponderance of long melodic vowels, and an "sh" alliteration (lines 3-6). Then she effects a contrast through the geese analogy by the use of a harsh alliteration and shortened vowels (lines 6-7). How can you enhance this language? How can you present the contrast?

The technique of handling the repetition of the thesis "Euclid alone has looked on Beauty bare" (lines 1 and 11) should not be left to chance. How will you manage it?

c   Verse drama

Porphyria's Lover

BY ROBERT BROWNING

The rain set early in to-night,
   The sullen wind was soon awake,
It tore the elm-tops down for spite,
   And did its worst to vex the lake:
   I listened with heart fit to break.   5
When glided in Porphyria; straight
   She shut the cold out and the storm,
And kneeled and made the cheerless grate
   Blaze up, and all the cottage warm;
   Which done, she rose and from her form   10
Withdrew the dripping cloak and shawl,
   And laid her soiled gloves by, untied
Her hat and let the damp hair fall,
   And, last, she sat down by my side
   And called me. When no voice replied,   15
She put my arm about her waist,
   And made her smooth white shoulder bare,
And all her yellow hair displaced
   And, stooping, made my cheek lie there,
   And spread, o'er all, her yellow hair,   20
Murmuring how she loved me—she
   Too weak, for all her heart's endeavour,
To set its struggling passion free
   From pride, and vainer ties dissever,
   And give herself to me for ever.   25
But passion sometimes would prevail,
   Nor could tonight's gay feast restrain
A sudden thought of one so pale
   For love of her, and all in vain:

So, she was come through wind and rain.   30
Be sure I looked up at her eyes
    Happy and proud; at last I knew
Porphyria worshipped me; surprise
    Made my heart swell, and still it grew
    While I debated what to do.   35
That moment she was mine, mine, fair,
    Perfectly pure and good: I found
A thing to do, and all her hair
    In one long yellow string I wound
    Three times her little throat around,   40
And strangled her. No pain felt she;
    I am quite sure she felt no pain.
As a shut bud that holds a bee,
    I warily open her lids: again
    Laughed the blue eyes without a stain.   45
And I untightened next the tress
    About her neck; her cheek once more
Blushed bright beneath my burning kiss:
    I propped her head up as before,
    Only, this time my shoulder bore   50
Her head, which droops upon it still:
    The smiling rosy little head,
So glad it has its utmost will,
    That all it scorned at once is fled,
    And I, its love, am gained instead!   55
Porphyria's love: she guessed not how
    Her darling one wish would be heard.
And thus we sit together now,
    And all night long we have not stirred,
    And yet God has not said a word!   60

Suggested interpretation

The study of this poem would be a field day for the clinical
psychologist. Fortunately for the lover of literature this is a

dramatic poem and not a case study. We have imagination here
rather than an accurate technical diagnosis, we have design rather
than a dull coverage of detail, and we have a universality of appeal
rather than a gory story leveled at sensation lovers. Pride, selfish-
ness, insecurity, self-deception, rationalization are the character
traits of the protagonist by whom human nature is mirrored quite
accurately.

The basic structure of the poem is simple: the setting, the en-
trance, the love making, the resolution, the killing, the mock love
making, the waiting. Each part is described with vivid imagery
but within short iambic tetrameter lines closely knit together with
recurrent rhyme. There are no impassioned speeches; there is a
minimum of violence.

Can you construct an interpretative pattern to fit this structure?
Can you suggest the wildness of the gale without making too much
noise? Can you introduce a sense of foreboding as the love making
does not seem to proceed quite right? Can you describe the death
scene, with skillful restraint? Can you re-enact the love scene as
something tenderly macaber? Can you interpret the discordant
quiet and peace of the conclusion?

There are details of interpretation to work out even though
there is probably no radical change from part to part or even
within the parts. You need to contrast the harshness of the storm
with the softness of Porphyria's movements. And you need to
contrast the warmth of the girl with the coldness of the man. If
the first real indication of uneasiness appears in line 15, how
might that phrase be made to stand out? Unless you are sure of
your control there may be too crude a progression from lines 37
to 41. Shall line 42 be an exact echo of line 41? Probably not.
Probably there is here a real opportunity to shift from plot un-
foldment to character revelation. How does the last line, 60, fit
into the whole?

You might be seated while reading this poem. The protagonist
was sitting. You might look at your listeners quite steadily. This
is certainly a dramatic reading. We should see the character in
you rather than through you (even though you are a female).
But any attempt to act (to wind hair in the air, for instance)
would be a mistake. Suggest, and suggest with the utmost restraint. Then let horror prevail!

d A lyric

The Dreame

JOHN DONNE

Deare love, for nothing lesse than thee
Would I have broke this happy dreame,
       It was a theame
For reason, much too strong for phantasie,
Therefore thou wakd'st me wisely; yet   5
My Dreame thou brok'st not, but continued'st it,
Thou art so true, that thoughts of thee suffice
To make dreames truths; and fables histories;
Enter these armes, for since thou thoughtst it best,
Not to dreame all my dreame, let's act the rest.   10

As lightning, or a Tapers light,
Thine eyes, and not thy noise wak'd mee;
       Yet I thought thee
(For thou lovest truth) an Angell, at first sight,
But when I saw thou sawest my heart,   15
And knew'st my thoughts, beyond an Angels art,
When thou knew'st what I dreamt, when thou knew'st when
Excesse of joy would wake me, and cam'st then,
I must confesse, it could not chuse but bee
Prophane, to thinke thee anything but thee.   20

Comming and staying show'd thee, thee,
But rising makes me doubt, that now,
       Thou art not thou.
That love is weake, where feare's as strong as hee;
'Tis not all spirit, pure, and brave,   25
If mixture it of *Feare, Shame, Honor,* have.
Perchance as torches which must ready bee,
Men light and put out, so thou deal'st with mee;
Thou cam'st to kindle, goest to come; then I
Will dreame that hope againe, but else would die.   30

Suggested interpretation

In the seventeenth century men were disciplined in manners and in love. Anyone who would let his heart rule his head was either a fool or was deliberately taking a holiday.

John Donne was no fool; in this love lyric he managed to contrive an intellectually pleasing "conceit." It would be a grievous mistake therefore to read sheer unrestrained romanticism in the poem; it would be ludicrous to wax sentimental in oral interpretation.

There are romantic elements here, however. And the magnificent combination of imagery with restraint makes this a love poem of outstanding beauty. We merely wish to make clear, that if his mistress did *not* return he would certainly not die—and they both knew it!

Might the basic interpretation conform rather closely to the symmetry of thought and structure? The thought is divided into three stanzas—the awakening, the comprehension, and the uncertainty. The structure is original. The first five verses of each stanza are irregular in length and (except for the fourth) are shorter than the rest. The last five are all in iambic pentameter.

Can you so contrive a technique of interpretation that the thought units are rendered distinct one from the other? Does the stanza structure enable you to locate each climax?

As for mood, do not the stateliness and delicacy of the meter, coupled with the fact that the conceits are artfully rather than sentimentally conceived, indicate the need for precision, restraint, and finesse?

Before working out more details of interpretation you should be aware of certain technical factors. The rhyme scheme is *a b b a c c d d e e*. Do you intend to conform or will you choose to use modern pronunciation? Then there is not only the inflectional form, "—est," for the second person singular, but it is contracted, as indicated by the apostrophe. One effect of this is to present some difficult sound combinations (see lines 5-6 especially). Then there are unusual word sequences with inversions of customary word order and omissions of functional words. The third stanza contains several of these. For example, is "Honor" (line 26) the subject of "have" or the object of "of"? Finally, can you trace the exact thought sequence in the sentence from lines 15 to 20?

Would not the reading of lines 5 and 6 with a relatively slow tempo so that the sounds can be made with extreme accuracy coupled with the reading of lines 7 and 8 with a slow tempo so that the music of the full vowel sounds can be appreciated result in a pattern of contrasting duration (short *vs* long vowels) that will subtly reflect the tender mood of awakening?

How would you pattern the progression of the second stanza? You will certainly have to watch the relation of sense stress to metrical accent. Stressing both "saw's" (line 15) would be confusing. How about both "thee's" (line 20)? And how would you handle all of the "when's" and the "then"? Will there be a build up in tempo and intensity and pitch level? Will a change in quality enhance the climax of lines 19-20?

Would you be intrigued with a pattern of progression in the third stanza that would be the inverse of the preceding one—a gradual diminuendo? Do you notice a similarity in the vowel length contrast of lines 29 and 30 similar to that mentioned regarding the first stanza?

Please prepare with care the reading of the last four words. You must not be maudlin, but you must not break the spell. There is an intensity of restraint here that calls for little volume but most exacting control. This line alone can make your interpretation a thing of beauty.

e **Free verse**

Hurt Hawks *

ROBINSON JEFFERS

I

The broken pillar of the wing jags from the clotted shoulder,
The wing trails like a banner in defeat,
No more to use the sky forever but live with famine
And pain a few days: cat nor coyote
Will shorten the week of waiting for death, there is game without   5
        talons.
He stands under the oak-bush and waits
The lame feet of salvation; at night he remembers freedom

And flies in a dream, the dawns ruin it.

He is strong and pain is worse to the strong, incapacity is
        worse.

The curs of the day come and torment him   10

At distance, no one but death the redeemer will humble that
        head,

The intrepid readiness, the terrible eyes.

The wild God of the world is sometimes merciful to those

That ask mercy, not often to the arrogant.

You do not know him, you communal people, or you have   15
        forgotten him;

Intemperate and savage, the hawk remembers him;

Beautiful and wild, the hawks, and men that are dying,
        remember him.

II

I'd sooner, except the penalties, kill a man than a hawk;
        but the great redtail

Had nothing left but unable misery

From the bone too shattered for mending, the wing that trailed   20
        under his talons when he moved.

We had fed him six weeks, I gave him freedom,

He wandered over the foreland hill and returned in the evening,
        asking for death,

Not like a beggar, still eyed with old

Implacable arrogance. I gave him the lead gift in the twilight.
        What fell was relaxed,   25

Owl-downy, soft feminine feathers; but what

Soared: the fierce rush: the night-herons by the flooded river
        cried fear at its rising

Before it was quite unsheathed from reality.

Suggested interpretation

The locale of this poem like so many others by Robinson
Jeffers is the wild, barren, sparsely settled region where the west-

ern slopes of the Coast Range dip into the Pacific Ocean from Point Lobos to Point Sur. Jeffers, writing in his isolated stone tower beside his home at Carmel, lays bare the essentials of beauty and ugliness, strength and weakness, warmth and coldness that he finds in both man and beast in this region about him.

It is necessary to study some phrases and expressions for exact meaning, such as ". . . and waits the lame feet of salvation" (lines 6-7) and "you communal people" (line 15). Should night-herons ordinarily fear hawks (line 27)?

This is free verse and it is challenging. It is free only in the sense that it is not cast in a metrical pattern. But it is not free from an exact rhythmic pattern which should be followed in the interpretation.

Then there is the basic pattern of mood and thought.

Through the figure of synecdoche (in this case, part for whole) Jeffers introduces the hawk to us—hurt beyond hope. The hawk dreams of health, then awakens to reality to resume the attitude of defiance. Then comes reflection and observation on the philosophy of defiance. A definite break follows: the personal resolve of the man to liberate and then to shoot the bird. Finally there is the breath-taking resolution—the falling of the feathers, and the rising of the spirit.

Just what *is* the basic pattern? Should narrative or philosophy or imagery prevail? Should they intermingle? Should there be definite shifts at the main divisions outlined above? How should you relate the unity of the whole to the diversity of the parts? It might be suggested that you read with the unhurried dignity of the hurt hawk itself. If you do you will notice a beat akin to the stateliness of blank verse without its regularity.

Pay careful attention to details or you will be unable to design interpretative schemes that will encompass them all. For instance, notice the onomatopoeic force of "jags" in the first line, surrounded by the stopped consonants in "broken pillar" and "clotted shoulder." Again there is onomatopoeia in "fierce rush" (line 26). Use your voice well to enhance the pictures evoked by "The curs of the day come and torment him," "intemperate and savage," "too shattered for mending," "implacable arrogance," "Owl-downy."

The details of interpretation for the most part will be concerned with making contrasts, in setting part next to part. How, for instance, would you set ". . . the hawk remembers him," (lines 16-17) in juxtaposition to "and men that are dying remember him"? How would you effect a transition from line 20 to line 21?

And how can you read lines 26 to 28 so that they make a fitting ending?

We remark that this poem is most difficult to read with justice done. You need sensitivity, you need timing, but above all you need discipline. To read this well may require such firm control, such exactness of interpretation, such expenditure of nerve energy that when you have finished you will be near exhaustion. But you will be satisfied. Try it. The poem is a challenge.

f Free verse

Boy and Father *

CARL SANDBURG

The boy Alexander understands his father to be a famous lawyer.

The leather law books of Alexander's father fill a room like hay in a barn.

Alexander has asked his father to let him build a house like brick-layers build, a house with walls and roofs made of big leather law books.

The rain beats on the windows
And the raindrops run down the window glass
And the raindrops slide off the green blinds down the siding.

The boy Alexander dreams of Napoleon in John C. Abbott's history, Napoleon the grand and lonely man wronged, Napoleon in his life wronged and in his memory wronged.

The boy Alexander dreams of the cat Alice saw, the cat fading off into the dark and leaving the teeth of its Cheshire smile lighting the gloom.

Buffaloes, blizzards, way down in Texas, in the panhandle of Texas snuggling close to New Mexico,

These creep into Alexander's dreaming by the window when his father talks with strange men about land down in Deaf Smith County.

Alexander's father tells the strange men: Five years ago we ran a Ford out on the prairie and chased antelopes.

Only once or twice in a long while has Alexander heard his father say "my first wife" so-and-so and such-and-such.
A few times softly the father has told Alexander, "Your mother . . . was a beautiful woman . . . but we won't talk about her."
Always Alexander listens with a keen listen when he hears his father mention "my first wife" or "Alexander's mother."

Alexander's father smokes a cigar and the Episcopal rector smokes a cigar and the words come often: mystery of life, mystery of life.
These two come into Alexander's head blurry and gray while the rain beats on the windows and the raindrops run down the window glass and the raindrops slide off the green blinds and down the siding.
These and: There is a God, there must be a God, how can there be rain or sun unless there is a God:

So from the wrongs of Napoleon and the Cheshire cat smile on to the buffaloes and blizzards of Texas and on to his mother and to God, so the blurry gray rain dreams of Alexander have gone on five minutes, maybe ten, keeping slow easy time to the raindrops on the window glass and the raindrops sliding off the green blinds and down the siding.

Suggested interpretation

The failure in communication between Alexander and his father reveals the immeasurable gulf between them. There is not only a difference of years but of interests and values. Alexander attempts to cross the gulf in the opening lines but it is not possible.

The opportunity to work out an interpretative technique that corresponds to the form of Sandburg's poem is challenging. What vocal techniques will reproduce the dreams of the boy, the mundane interests of the father, his ineffectual attempts to talk of his first wife, the desperate need of Alexander to affirm God's existence, the final review of the impressions rushing through consciousness, and the raindrop refrain symbolizing frustration, impasse, loneliness?

What feeling tones might suggest the dreams of the boy and the expressions of the father? How will you read the refrain? Would there be monotony of tempo and intensity there? Would you read the line beginning: "There is a God—" with extreme rapidity and jerkiness, or would you read it slowly, fervently, wistfully?

Watch for contrasts and similarities; watch for the breaks in thought and mood, and decide carefully just what you can do with your voice to make a perfect oral facsimile of the structure and the symmetry of this poem.*

g Humorous verse

A Seaside Romance †

DON MARQUIS

"My name," I said, "is Peleg Doddleding,
And Doddleding has been my name since birth."
And having told the girl this shameful thing
I bowed my head and waited for her mirth.

She did not laugh. I looked at her, and she,   5
With wistful gladness in her yellow eyes,
Swept with her gradual gaze the mocking sea.
Then dried her gaze and swept the scornful skies.

I thought perhaps she had not heard aright.
"My name," I said again, "is Doddleding!"   10

* This poem appears again in the lecture recital, pp. 167-9.
† From *Noah an' Jonah an' Cap'n John Smith* by Don Marquis. Copyright 1921, D. Appleton & Company. Reprinted by permission of the publishers Appleton-Century-Crofts, Inc.

Thinking she would reply, "Ah, then, good night;
No love of mine round such a name could cling!"

We'd met upon the beach an hour before,
And our loves leapt together, flame and flame.
I loved, She loved. We loved. "She'll love no more,"   15
I moaned, "when she learns Doddleding's my name."

She was not beautiful, nor did she seem
The sort of person likely to be good;
Her outcast manner 'twas that bade me dream
If *any one* could stand my name she could.   20

She seemed a weakly sentimental thing.
Vicious, no doubt, and dull and somewhat wried.
I said once more, "I'm Mister Doddleding!"
Feebly she smiled. I saw she had no pride.

The westering sun above the ocean shook   25
With ecstasy, the flushed sea shook beneath . . .
I trembled too . . . She smiled! . . . and one long look
Showed something queer had happened to her teeth.

O world of gladness! World of gold and flame!
"She loves me, then, in spite of all!" I cried.   30
"Though Peleg Doddleding is still my name,
Yet Peleg Doddleding has found a bride!"

I stroked her hair . . . I found it was a wig . . .
And as I slipped upon her hand the ring
She said, "*My* name is Effie Muddlesnig—   35
Oh, thank you! *Thank* you! Mister Doddleding!"

In all the world she was the only one
For me, and I for her . . . lives touch and pass,
And then, some day beneath a westering sun,
We find our own! One of her eyes is glass.   40

Suggested interpretation

If this is read well your audience will love it. But don't think it has no literary value because it is funny. This is good satire. It is a delightful take off on the second-rate love lyric. Don Marquis has fun with the consciously clever poet who strives for precious style (lines 7-8, 25-26, 37-39).

The basic problem consists of relating the sensible to the absurd and the sentimental to the comic. Your interpretation may approach impersonation or it may be impersonally classic, but you do have to pretend to be serious—at times.

There are genuine technical difficulties: the repetition of "Doddleding" three times, and the introduction of dialogue (male and female) in the midst of the narration, but the real problem is to suggest the humor with a light touch.

The details of interpretation follow the general pattern. In line 6, the word "yellow" should destroy the "beauty" of the rest. Lines 13-14 can be ecstatic, but the Latin conjugation appearing in line 15 should bring us out of the ecstasy immediately. The double entendre of lines 17-18 is hard to manage. Consider the onomatopoeic effect of "vicious" (line 22). Then there is the shift in intensity and quality and sublimity from line 25 to "I trembled too," etc., until you have your final chance to utter the "lofty" sentiments of lines 37-39 in such a manner that you almost attain to the heights of the best soap opera. Then comes the last line. Don Marquis is delightful reading.

VII

THE LECTURE RECITAL

The true artist appreciates and shares his appreciation with others. You, the interpretative artist, will do likewise. Oftentimes the richest experiences are shared in the classroom. But the classroom situation is, for the most part, a learning situation. There you become acquainted with good literature. You acquire taste and discrimination in your selection, you learn to be painstaking in assimilating the material, and you learn to communicate the thoughts and feelings of others as naturally and as easily as if they were your own. The time will come, however, when you will have the opportunity to give a finished performance of oral reading either to the class or in public.

On such an occasion, if you choose to read a single work, such as Hemingway's *The Old Man and the Sea,* or portions of a longer work, such as Stephen Vincent Benét's *John Brown's Body,* or Anne Morrow Lindbergh's *Gift from the Sea* you will need to prepare a brief introduction so that the audience will be properly prepared for what is coming. Possibly someone else will give the introduction. But if you choose to read several selections from the same author or selections from different authors around a central theme, you will need to pay considerable attention to your introduction and to the remarks you may need to make during the course of your reading. We call this sort of reading—the combination of interpretative reading and appropriate remarks by the reader—the *lecture recital.*

The lecture recital affords you the opportunity for being a creative as well as a re-creative artist. It is a reading with a purpose, and, if well done, should leave a lasting impression upon you as well as upon your audience.

Whether your lecture recital consists of a number of selections from one author or whether you select from a number of authors that which will develop a theme, you will do well to write out your introduction and continuing remarks, inserting them in the script at the appropriate place.

A finished reading should be "memorized" to the extent that you achieve complete freedom from the printed page. You should be as free from the need to translate the printed word into the spoken word as the linguist is in his translation of one language into another. And you should be free to look at your audience or to look away from them according to your purpose and the nature of your material.

We are including a number of lecture recitals that have actually been given by students in oral interpretation classes. They are presented not because they are considered to be outstanding, but because they illustrate the possibilities in this field. They have been prepared to conform to a time limit which, under certain circumstances, becomes an important factor. Cut or eliminate as necessity dictates, but never rush. Remember that the clock ticks off seconds of silence as well as of sound.

Read these recitals and then consider what you yourself would like to do. It will be most satisfying if you can conclude the study of the oral reading of literature with a lecture recital.*

Thomas Wolfe
The Great Searcher

SALLY COTTON

In my opinion Thomas Wolfe is one of the most fascinating figures in twentieth-century American literature. He was a man of passionate extremes: one moment he would be dwelling in ecstatic delight and in the next be plunged into the depths of despair. He was a romanticist, and he had the typical artistic temperament.

He wrote of the things he saw about him in a delicate, sensitive, and poetic manner. He was fascinated by life, and could see, with what might be termed an inner eye, a personal meaning in the smallest, most commonplace things that are normally taken for granted. Thus he wrote

---

* There is no reason, of course, why you should not choose a single selection from any of these recitals to read as a separate class assignment.

The Way Things Are *

This is the way things are.
Here is the grass,
So green and so coarse, so sweet and delicate,
But with some brown rubble in it.

There are the houses all along the street,
The concrete blocks of walls,
Somehow so dreary,
Ugly, yet familiar,
The slate roofs and the shingles,
The lawns, the hedges and the gables,
The backyards with their accidental structures
Of so many little and familiar things
As hen houses, barns.

All common and familiar as my breath,
All accidental as the strings of blind chance,
Yet all somehow fore-ordered as a destiny:
The way they are,
Because
They are the way they are!

This fragile quality reflected in his handling of material is again perfectly exemplified in the following short selection

Fountain †

On the Square
The slackened fountain
Dropped a fat spire of freezing water
Into its thickening rim of ice.

---

* From *The Web and the Rock* by Thomas Wolfe. Reprinted by permission of Harper and Brothers.

† Reprinted with the permission of Charles Scribner's Sons from *Look Homeward, Angel,* by Thomas Wolfe (Copyright 1929 Charles Scribner's Sons; renewal copyright © 1957 Edward C. Aswell, Administrator, C.T.A. of the Estate of Thomas Wolfe and Fred W. Wolfe).

In summer, a tall spire
Blown in blue sheets of spray.
When they turned it down,
It wilted—
That was like a fountain, too.

Often when I read something by Wolfe, I come across a selection that seems to leap off the paper at me and smack me in the face, saying—"This is true! You've always known this but could never express it in so many words."—And for a few moments I am stunned and amazed because of his remarkable ability to interpret abstract concepts in such concrete terms. Such a thing happened to me when I read

Pity *

Pity, more than any other feeling,
Is a "learned" emotion;
A child will have it least of all.
Pity comes
From the infinite accumulations of man's memory,
From the anguish, pain, and suffering of life,
From the full deposit of experience,
From the forgotten faces, the lost men,
And from the million strange and haunting visages
Of time.

Pity comes upon the nick of time
And stabs us like a knife.
Its face is thin and dark and burning,
And it has come before we know it,
Gone before we can grasp or capture it;
It leaves a shrewd, deep wound,
But a bitter subtle one,
And it always comes most keenly
From a little thing.

* From *The Web and the Rock* by Thomas Wolfe. Reprinted by permission of Harper and Brothers.

It comes without herald or a cause we can determine,
At some moment in our lives when we are
Far and lost from all the scenes that pity comes from;
And how, why, where it comes
We cannot say.
But suddenly in the city—
In the great and million-footed city—
Pity comes to us at evening
When the dust and fury of another city day is over,
And we lean upon the sills of evening
In an ancient life.

Then pity comes to us;
We will remember children's voices of long ago,
The free, full shout of sudden, gleeful laughter
From a child that we once knew,
Full of exulting innocence,
The songs we sang on summer porches long ago,
A note of pride in our mother's voice
And her grave, worn eyes of innocence
As she boasted of a little thing.

Oh then will pity come,
Strange, sudden pity
With its shrewd knife and the asp of time
To stab us
With a thousand wordless, lost, forgotten,
Little things!

And how, where, why it came
We cannot say,
But we feel pity now
For all men who have ever lived upon the earth . . .
And . . . all men yet unborn, and yet to live
Who will come after us!

It seems paradoxical that a man who could so clearly see truths about life and find meaning in little things should feel himself to be so lost and alone in an alien world. He was, according to my title, "The Great Searcher." And his "Great Search" was for a place for himself in the world and for a father image. This search is revealed again and again in his works. It is the theme of the oft quoted passage,

A Stone, A Leaf, A Door *

. . . A stone, a leaf, an unfound door;
Of a stone, a leaf, a door.
And all of the forgotten faces.

Naked and alone we came into exile.
In her dark womb
We did not know our mother's face;
From the prison of her flesh have we come
Into the unspeakable and incommunicable prison
Of this earth.

Which of us has known his brother?
Which of us has looked into his father's heart?
Which of us has not remained forever prison-pent?
Which of us is not a stranger and alone?

O waste of loss, in the hot mazes, lost,
Among bright stars
On this most weary unbright cinder, lost!
Remembering speechlessly
We seek the great forgotten language,
The lost lane-end into heaven,
A stone, a leaf, an unfound door.

And he was afraid of death—afraid of it because he felt he would not have the time to complete his search; that he would die "lonely and in exile," just as he had come into the world. Thus, his works contain references to the passage of time, such as,

* Reprinted with the permission of Charles Scribner's Sons from *Look Homeward, Angel,* by Thomas Wolfe (Copyright 1929 Charles Scribner's Sons; renewal copyright © 1957 Edward C. Aswell, Administrator, C.T.A. of the Estate of Thomas Wolfe and Fred W. Wolfe).

Stranger than a Dream *

And time still passing . . . passing like a leaf . . .
Time passing, fading like a flower . . .
Time passing like a river flowing . . .
Time passing as men pass
Who will never come back again.

And again—Notice how time takes on the definite form of a river in,

Full with the Pulse of Time *

Full with the pulse of time it flows there,
Full with the pulse of all men, living, sleeping,
Dying, waking,
[The river] will flow there,
Full with the billion dark and secret moments of our lives
It flows there.
Filled with all the hope, the madness
And the passion of our youth
It flows by us, by us, by us,
To the sea!

In the next selection his two attitudes about death and time are intricately woven together, and he asks the question, "Why are we here? How can I complete my search when life moves by so rapidly and death seems always closely impending?" Once more he uses poetic imagery in which the wind symbolizes time.

To Keep Time With *

What is this dream of time,
This strange and bitter miracle of living?

Is it the wind that drives the leaves
Down bare paths fleeing?
Is it the storm-wild flight of furious days,
The storm-swift passing of the million faces,
All lost, forgotten, vanished as a dream?
Is it the wind that howls above the earth,
Is it the wind that drives all things before its lash,
Is it the wind that drives all men like dead ghosts fleeing?
Is it the one red leaf that strains there on the bough
And that forever will be fleeing?
All things are lost and broken in the wind:
The dry leaves scamper down the path before us,
In their swift-winged dance of death
The dead souls flee along before us,
Driven with rusty scuffle
Before the fury of the demented wind.

It seems to me that Thomas Wolfe's great tragedy is that he was searching in the wrong place for his "father." He was looking for a spiritual security among men, rather than turning to God which might have been the more logical direction. He well knew man's defects and impurities, but still he had a burning, almost fanatical faith in the human race. The following excerpt begins by violently and pessimistically criticizing man and ends in a final note of triumph. In the last analysis the mortal is a beautiful and perfect thing, regardless of his faults!

This Is Man *

For what is man?

First a child, soft-boned,
Unable to support itself on its rubbery legs . . .
That howls and laughs by turns,

* From *You Can't Go Home Again* by Thomas Wolfe, Copyright 1934, 1937, 1938, 1939, 1940 by Maxwell Perkins as Executor. Reprinted by permission of Harper and Brothers.

Cries for the moon . . .
A beloved fool.

After that, a boy,
Hoarse and loud before his companions,
But afraid of the dark;
Will beat the weaker and avoid the stronger . . .
Would rather die than not out-try
And out-dare his companions,
Wants to beat them and always to win . . .
Boasts of his victories
And will never own defeat.

Then the youth . . .
Begins to think about his clothes,
Becomes a fop, greases his hair,
Smokes cigarettes with a dissipated air,
Reads novels, and writes poetry on the sly . . .
He knows hate, love, and jealousy;
He is cowardly and foolish,
He cannot endure to be alone;
He lives in a crowd, thinks with the crowd,
Is afraid to be marked off from his fellows
By an eccentricity.
He joins clubs and is afraid of ridicule;
He is bored and unhappy
And wretched most of the time.
There is a great cavity in him,
He is dull.

Then the man:
He is busy,
He is full of plans and reasons,
He has work.
He gets children,
Buys and sells small packets of everlasting earth,

Intrigues against his rivals,
Is exultant when he cheats them.
He wastes his little three-score years and ten
In spendthrift and inglorious living;
From his cradle to his grave
He scarcely sees
The sun or moon or stars;
He is unconscious of the immortal sea and earth;
He talks of the future
And he wastes it as it comes . . .

This is man:
A writer of books, a putter-downer of words,
A painter of pictures,
A maker of ten thousand philosophies . . .
Yet in the billion books upon the shelves
There is not one that can tell him
How to draw a single fleeting breath
In peace and comfort.
He makes histories of the universe,
He directs the destiny of nations,
But he does not know his own history,
And he cannot direct his own destiny
With dignity or wisdom
For ten consecutive minutes

This is man:
For the most part
A foul, wretched abominable creature,
A packet of decay,
A bundle of degenerating tissues . . .
A thing that kills and murders in a mob
Or in the dark,
Loud and full of brag surrounded by his fellows,
But without the courage of a rat, alone . . .

Yes, this is man,
And it is impossible to say the worst of him
For the record of his obscene existence,
His baseness, lust, cruelty, and treachery,
Is illimitable.

His life is also full of toil, tumult and suffering.
His days are mainly composed
Of a million idiot repetitions—
In goings and comings along hot streets,
In sweatings and freezings,
In the senseless accumulation of fruitless tasks . . .

This is man,
Who, if he can remember ten golden moments of
    joy and happiness
Out of all his years,
Ten moments unmarked by care . . .
Has power to lift himself with his expiring breath,
And say, "I have lived upon this earth
And known glory!"

This is man,
And one wonders why he wants to live at all.
A third of his life is lost and deadened under sleep;
Another third is given to a sterile labor;
A sixth is spent in all his goings and his comings . . .
How much of him is left
To look upon the everlasting earth?
How much of him is left for glory
And the makings of great songs? . . .

Yet if the gods could come here
To a desolate, deserted earth
Where only the ruin of man's cities remained,
Where only a few marks and carvings of his hand

Were legible upon his broken tablets,
Where only a wheel lay rusting in the desert sand,
A cry would burst out of their hearts
And they would say:
"He lived and he was here!"

Behold his works:

He needed speech to ask for bread—and he had Christ!
He needed songs to sing in battle—and he had Homer!
He needed words to curse his enemies—
And he had Dante, he had Voltaire, he had Swift!
He needed cloth to cover up his hairless, puny flesh
    against the seasons—
And he wove the robes of Solomon . . .
He was born to creep upon the earth—
And he made great wheels,
He sent great engines thundering down the rails,
He launched great wings into the air,
He put great ships upon the angry sea!

Plagues wasted him,
And cruel wars destroyed his strongest sons,
But fire, flood, and famine could not quench him.

For there is one belief, one faith,
That is man's glory, his triumph, his immortality—
And that is his belief in life.
Man loves life,
And loving life, hates death,
And because of this he is great, he is glorious,
He is beautiful, and his beauty is everlasting . . .

Thus it is impossible to scorn this creature.
For out of his strong belief in life,
This puny man made love.

At his best,
He *is* love.
Without him
There can be no love,
No hunger, no desire.

But there is a mystery about Thomas Wolfe that we may never solve. Throughout all of his lyrical, beautiful, and sensitive writing, there exists, as I've tried to point out, a constant emphasis on the quick passing of time, on the fear of death, and on a fantastic search for a father. There is no indication that his spiritual needs were ever completely satisfied, but critics often wonder now if Wolfe, "The Great Searcher," did in the end turn from his faith in the mortal, to the security of a belief in the immortal—in God. There is only one passage in Wolfe which would lead them to think in this manner. It is the one in which he accepts death as something ultimately good.

Toward Which *

Something has spoken to me in the night,
Burning the tapers of the waning year;
Something has spoken in the night,
And told me I shall die, I know not where.

Saying:
"To lose the earth you know, for greater knowing;
To lose the life you have, for greater life;
To leave the friends you loved, for greater loving;
To find a land more kind than home, more large than
    earth—

"—Whereon the pillars of this earth are founded,
Toward which the conscience of the world is tending—
A wind is rising, and the rivers flow."

* From *You Can't Go Home Again* by Thomas Wolfe. Copyright 1934, 1937, 1938, 1939, 1940 by Maxwell Perkins as Executor. Reprinted by permission of Harper and Brothers.

Communication

SHIRLEY AHERN

"Which of us has not remained forever a stranger and alone?" Isn't it remarkable that man, a basically gregarious animal, can talk and talk and talk and never communicate? All too often a gulf seems to open between two human beings when they want to speak to one another. Such is the situation in Muriel Rukeyser's,

Effort at Speech Between Two People *

Speak to me. Take my hand. What are you now?
I will tell you all. I will conceal nothing.
When I was three, a little child read a story about a rabbit
who died, in the story, and I crawled under a chair:
a pink rabbit: it was my birthday, and a candle
burnt a sore spot on my finger, and I was told to be happy.

Oh, grow to know me. I am not happy. I will be open:
Now I am thinking of white sails against a sky like music,
like glad horns blowing, and birds tilting, and an arm about me.
There was one I loved who wanted to live, sailing.

Speak to me. Take my hand. What are you now:
When I was nine, I was fruitily sentimental,
fluid: and my widowed aunt played Chopin,
and I bent my head to the painted woodwork, and wept.
I want to be close to you. I would
link the minutes of my days close, somehow, to your days.

I am not happy. I will be open.
I have liked lamps in evening corners, and quiet poems.

* From *Theory of Flight* by Muriel Rukeyser. Copyright 1935 by Yale University. Copyright 1960 by Muriel Rukeyser.

There has been fear in my life. Sometimes I speculate
On what a tragedy his life was, really.

Take my hand. Fist my mind in your hand. What are you now?
When I was fourteen, I had dreams of suicide,
and I stood at a steep window, at sunset, hoping towards death:
If the light had not melted clouds and plains to beauty,
if light had not transformed that day, I would have leapt.
I am unhappy. I am lonely. Speak to me.

I will be open. I think he never loved me:
he loved the bright beaches, the little lips of foam
that ride small waves, he loved the veer of gulls:
he said with a gay mouth: I love you. Grow to know me.

What are you now: If we could touch one another,
If these our separate entities could come to grips,
clenched like a Chinese puzzle . . . yesterday
I stood in a crowded street that was live with people,
and no one spoke a word, and the morning shone.
Everyone silent, moving . . . Take my hand. Speak to me.

"Which of us has looked into his father's heart?" At a very
early age we begin to wonder about the people around us, what
they are thinking, what is important to them. And we wonder
about our parents, what are they really like? Carl Sandburg tells
us of this in

"Boy and Father" *

The boy Alexander understands his father to be a famous lawyer.

The leather law books of Alexander's father fill a room like hay
    in a barn.

* From *Smoke and Steel* by Carl Sandburg, copyright 1920 by Harcourt,
Brace & World, Inc.; renewed 1948 by Carl Sandburg. Reprinted by permission of the publishers.

Alexander has asked his father to let him build a house like brick-layers build, a house with walls and roofs made of big leather law books.

The rain beats on the windows
And the raindrops run down the window glass
And the raindrops slide off the green blinds down the siding.

The boy Alexander dreams of Napoleon in John C. Abbott's history, Napoleon the grand and lonely man wronged, Napoleon in his life wronged and in his memory wronged.

The boy Alexander dreams of the cat Alice saw, the cat fading off into the dark and leaving the teeth of its Cheshire smile lighting the gloom.

Buffaloes, blizzards, way down in Texas, in the panhandle of Texas snuggling close to New Mexico,
These creep into Alexander's dreaming by the window when his father talks with strange men about land down in Deaf Smith County.

Alexander's father tells the strange men: Five years ago we ran a Ford out on the prairie and chased antelopes.

Only once or twice in a long while has Alexander heard his father say "my first wife" so-and-so and such-and-such.
A few times softly the father has told Alexander, "Your mother . . . was a beautiful woman . . . but we won't talk about her."
Always Alexander listens with a keen listen when he hears his father mention "my first wife" or "Alexander's mother."

Alexander's father smokes a cigar and the Episcopal rector smokes a cigar and the words come often: mystery of life, mystery of life.
These two come into Alexander's head blurry and gray while the rain beats on the windows and the raindrops run down the window glass and the raindrops slide off the green blinds and down the siding.

These and: There is a God, there must be a God, how can there
be rain or sun unless there is a God:

So from the wrongs of Napoleon and the Cheshire cat smile on
to the buffaloes and blizzards of Texas and on to his mother
and to God, so the blurry gray rain dreams of Alexander
have gone on five minutes, maybe ten, keeping slow easy time
to the raindrops on the window glass and the raindrops sliding off the green blinds and down the siding.

For a reversal of the situation, a parent wonders about a son in
a tender study of a small child's duplicity in Tennessee Williams's

Which Is My Little Boy *

Which is my little boy, which is he,
Jean qui pleure ou Jean qui rit?

Jean qui rit is my delicate John,
The one with the Chinese slippers on,

Whose hobby horse in a single bound
Carries me back to native ground.

But Jean qui pleure is mysterieux
with sorrows older than Nashapur,

With all of the stars, and all of the moons
mirrored in little silver spoons.

Which is my little boy, which is he
Jean qui pleure ou Jean qui rit?

"Remembering speechlessly, we seek the lost lane-end into
Heaven," and perhaps two lovers find it unexpectedly, in "the
great forgotten language" of silence. E. E. Cummings's

somewhere i have never travelled *

somewhere i have never travelled, gladly beyond
any experience, your eyes have their silence:
in your most frail gesture are things which enclose me.
or which i cannot touch because they are too near

your slightest look easily will unclose me
though i have closed myself as fingers,
you open always petal by petal myself as Spring opens
(touching skillfully, mysteriously) her first rose

or if your wish be to close me, i and
my life will shut very beautifully, suddenly,
as when the heart of this flower imagines
the snow carefully everywhere descending;

nothing which we are to perceive in this world equals
the power of your intense fragility: whose texture
compels me with the color of its countries,
rendering death and forever with each breathing

(i do not know what it is about you that closes
and opens; only something in me understands
the voice of your eyes is deeper than all roses)
nobody, not even the rain, has such small hands

Drawing together all these threads of man's inability to communicate with others is Thomas Wolfe's prose poem with which
he begins *Look Homeward, Angel:*

A Stone, A Leaf, A Door †

. . . A stone, a leaf, an unfound door;
Of a stone, a leaf, a door.
And all of the forgotten faces.

* Copyright 1931, 1959, by E. E. Cummings. Reprinted from *Poems
1923-1954* by E. E. Cummings by permission of Harcourt, Brace & World,
Inc.
† Reprinted with the permission of Charles Scribner's Sons from *Look*

Naked and alone we came into exile.
In her dark womb
We did not know our mother's face;
From the prison of her flesh have we come
Into the unspeakable and incommunicable prison
Of this earth.

Which of us has known his brother?
Which of us has looked into his father's heart?
Which of us has not remained forever prison-pent?
Which of us is not a stranger and alone?

O waste of loss, in the hot mazes, lost,
Among bright stars
On this most weary unbright cinder, lost!
Remembering speechlessly
We seek the great forgotten language,
The lost lane-end into heaven,
A stone, a leaf, an unfound door.

Man in Two Hemispheres

JOYCE OSBORN

(Cuttings are indicated in the text by brackets)

Everyman's life has two hemispheres. There is the physical one,
which has for its pole the man's home. And there is the spiritual
one, which has for its pole the man's religion. Whether the home
and the religion work separately or together, in harmony or dis-
harmony, to greater or lesser degree, both pull at, change, and
individualize the man. Through the word pictures of some poets
and some prophets, I'd like to glimpse with you the interaction
of man with his physical and his spiritual environments.

The first group of readings will reveal the physical hemisphere. The surroundings which first affect a man are those of his home, both the shelter and the locale of that shelter where he lives. To what extent and by which ways he gains and maintains control of his home will influence his life. As we'll see from descriptions by three American poets, an industrial city, a secluded mountain, and an untamed prairie are each inhabited by men of a unique character.

I. The City

The city's inhabitants are generally efficient people. For within the skyscrapers where they work and dwell, they are free from occupation with the elements and are provided with facilities for social and economic progress. This home of the cityman is depicted by Carl Sandburg in "Skyscraper": *

By day the skyscraper looms in the smoke and sun and has a soul.
Prairie and valley, streets of the city, pour people into it and they
    mingle among its twenty floors and are poured out again back
    to the streets, prairies and valleys.
It is the men and women, boys and girls so poured in and out all
    day that give the building a soul of dreams and thoughts and
    memories.

[(Dumped in the sea or fixed in the desert, who would care for the
    building or speak its name or ask a policeman the way to it?)]

Elevators slide on their cables and tubes carry letters and parcels
    and iron pipes carry gas and water in and sewage out.
Wires climb with secrets, carry light and carry words, and tell
    terrors and profits and loves [—curses of men grappling
    plans of business and questions of women in plots of love].

Hour by hour the caissons reach down to the rock of the earth and
    hold the building to a turning planet.

* From *Chicago Poems* by Carl Sandburg. Copyright 1916 by Holt, Rinehart & Winston, Inc. Copyright 1944 by Carl Sandburg. Reprinted by permission of the publishers.

Hour by hour the girders play as ribs and reach out and hold together the stone walls and floors.

[Hour by hour the hand of the mason and the stuff of the mortar
clinch the pieces and parts to the shape an architect voted.
Hour by hour the sun and the rain, the air and the rust, and the
press of time running into centuries, play on the building inside
and out and use it.]

Men who sunk the pilings and mixed the mortar are laid in graves
where the wind whistles a wild song without words
[And so are men who strung the wires and fixed the pipes and
tubes and these who saw it rise floor by floor.
Souls of them all are here, even the hod carrier begging at back
doors hundreds of miles away and the bricklayer who went to
state's prison for shooting another man while drunk.]
(One man fell from a girder and broke his neck at the end of a
straight plunge—he is here—his soul has gone into the stones
of the building.)

On the office doors from tier to tier—hundreds of names and each
name standing for a face written across with a dead child, a
passionate lover, a driving ambition for a million dollar business
or a lobster's ease of life.

Behind the signs on the doors they work and the walls tell nothing
from room to room.
Ten-dollar-a-week stenographers take letters from corporation
officers, lawyers, efficiency engineers, and tons of letters go
bundled from the building to all ends of the earth.
Smiles and tears of each office girl go into the soul of the building
just the same as the master-men who rule the building.

Hands of clocks turn to noon hours and each floor empties its
men and women who go away and eat and come back to work.
Toward the end of the afternoon all work slackens and all jobs
go slower as the people feel day closing on them.

One by one the floors are emptied . . . The uniformed elevator men are gone. Pails clang . . . Scrubbers work, talking in foreign tongues. Broom and water and mop clean from the floors human dust and spit, and machine grime of the day.

Spelled in electric fire on the roof are words telling miles of houses and people where to buy a thing for money. The sign speaks till midnight.

Darkness on the hallways. [Voices echo. Silence holds . . .] Watchmen walk slow from floor to floor and try the doors. Revolvers bulge from their hip pockets . . . [Steel safes stand in corners. Money is stacked in them.]

A young watchman leans at a window and sees [the lights of barges butting their way across a harbor, nets of red and white lanterns in a railroad yard, and] a span of gloom splashed with lines of white [and blurs of crosses and clusters over the sleeping city].

By night the skyscraper looms in the smoke and the stars and has a soul.

II. The Mountain

Life in the city is energetic, but on a remote mountain life is apt to be languid. For the tenant of the mountains knows that only with an easy-going pace can he enjoy the plants, birds, and animals which are the riches of his home. Such values are understood by Hill-Billy Jim, who is presented by Stephen Vincent Benét in "The Mountain Whippoorwill": *

Up in the mountains, it's lonesome all the time,
(Sof' win' slewin' thu' the sweet-potato vine).

Up in the mountains, it's lonesome for a child,
(Whippoorwills a-callin' when the sap runs wild).

* From *Selected Works of Stephen Vincent Benét*. Copyright 1925 by Stephen Vincent Benét. Copyright renewed 1953 by Rosemary Carr Benét. Reprinted by permission of Holt, Rinehart & Winston, Inc.

[Up in the mountains, mountains in the fog,
Everythin's as lazy as an old houn' dog.

Born in the mountains; never raised a pet,
Don't want nothin' an' never got it yet.]

Born in the mountains, lonesome-born,
Raised runnin' ragged thu' the cockleburrs and corn.

Never knew my pappy, mebbe never should.
Think he was a fiddle made of mountain laurel-wood.

Never had a mammy to teach me pretty-please.
Think she was a whippoorwill, a skitin' thu' the trees.

Never had a brother ner a whole pair of pants,
But when I start to fiddle, why, yuh got to start to dance!

Listen to my fiddle—Kingdom Come—Kingdom come!
Hear the frogs a-chunkin'—"Jug o' rum, Jug o' rum!"
Hear that mountain-whippoorwill be lonesome in the air,
An' I'll tell yuh how I travelled to the Essex County Fair.

Essex County has a mighty pretty fair,
All the smarty fiddlers from the South come there.

Elbows flyin' as they rosin up the bow
For the First Prize Contest in the Georgia Fiddler's Show.

Old Dan Wheeling, with his whiskers in his ears,
King-pin fiddler for nearly twenty years.

Big Tom Sargent, with his blue wall-eye,
An' Little Jimmy Weezer that can make a fiddle cry.

[All sittin' roun', spittin' high an' struttin' proud,
Listen, little whippoorwill, yuh better bug yore eyes:]

Tun-a-tun-a-tunin' while the jedges told the crowd
Them that got the mostest claps'd win the bestest prize.

Everybody waitin' for the first tweedle-dee,
When in comes a stumblin'—hill-billy me!

Bowed right pretty to the jedges and the rest,
Took a silver dollar from a hole inside my vest,
Plunked it on the table an' said, "There's my callin' card!
An' anyone that licks me—well, he's got to fiddle hard!"

Old Dan Wheeling, he was laughin' fit to holler,
Little Jimmy Weezer said, "There's one dead dollar!"
Big Tom Sargent had a yaller-toothy grin,
But I tucked my little whippoorwill spang underneath my chin,
An' petted it an' tuned it till the jedges said, "Begin!"

Big Tom Sargent was the first in line;
He could fiddle all the bugs off a sweet-potato vine.

[He could fiddle down a possum from a mile high tree.
He could fiddle up a whale from the bottom of the sea.]

Yuh could hear hands spankin' till they spanked each other raw,
When he finished variations on "turkey in the Straw."

Little Jimmy Weezer was the next to play;
He could fiddle all night, he could fiddle all day.

[He could fiddle chills, he could fiddle fever,
He could make a fiddle rustle like a lowland river.]

He could make a fiddle croon like a lovin' woman.
An' they clapped like thunder when he'd finished strummin'.

Then came the ruck of the bob tailed fiddlers,
The let's go easies, the fair to middlers.

They got their claps an' they lost their bicker,
An' settled back for some more corn licker.

And the crowd was tired of their no count squealing,
When out in the center steps Old Dan Wheeling.

He fiddled high and he fiddled low,
(Listen, little whippoorwill; yuh got to spread yore wings!)
[He fiddled with a cherrywood bow,
(Old Dan Wheeling's got bee honey in his strings.)]

He fiddled the wind by the lonesome moon,
He fiddled a most almighty tune.

He fiddled north an' he fiddled south,
He fiddled the heart right out of yore mouth.

[He fiddled here and he fiddled there.
He fiddled salvation everywhere.]

When he was finished, the crowd got loose,
(Whippoorwill, they's rain on yore breast.)
An' I sat there wonderin' "What's the Use?"
(Whippoorwill, fly home to yore nest.)

But I stood up pert an' I took my bow,
An' my fiddle on to my shoulder, so.

An'—they wasn't no crowd to get me fazed—
But I was alone where I was raised.

Up in the mountains, so still it makes yuh skeered.
Where God lies sleepin' in his big white beard.

[An' I heard the sound of the squirrel in the pine,
An' I heard the earth a-breathin' thu' the long night time.

They've fiddled the rose, an' they've fiddled the thorn,
But they haven't fiddled the mountain corn.

They've fiddled sinful an' fiddled moral,
But they haven't fiddled the brushwood laurel.

They've fiddled loud, an' they've fiddled still,
But they haven't fiddled the whippoorwill.]

I started off with a dump-diddle dump,
(*Oh, hell's broke loose in Georgia!*)
Skunk-cabbage growin' by the bee-gum stump,
(*Whippoorwill, yore singin' now!*)

[Oh, Georgia booze is mighty fine booze,
The best yuh ever poured yuh,
But it eats the soles right offen yore shoes,
Fer Hell's broke loose in Georgia.

My mother was a whippoorwill pert,
My father, he was lazy,
But I'm Hell broke loose in a new store shirt
To fiddle all Georgia crazy.]

Swing yore partners—up an' down the middle!
Sashay now—oh, listen to that fiddle!
Flapjacks flippin' on a red-hot griddle,
An' hell broke loose,
Hell broke loose,
Fire on the mountains—snakes in the grass.
Satan's here a-bilin'—oh, Lordy, let him pass!
Go down Moses, set my people free,
Pop goes the weasel thu' the old Red Sea!

Jonah sittin' on a hickory-bough,
Up jumps a whale —an' where's yore prophet now?
Rabbit in the pea-patch, possum in the pot,
Try an' stop my fiddle, now my fiddle's gettin' hot!
[Whippoorwill, singin' thu' the mountain hush,
Whippoorwill, shoutin' from the burnin' bush,
Whippoorwill, cryin' in the stable door,
Sing to-night as yuh never sung before!
Hell's broke loose like a stompin' mountain shoat,
Sing till you bust the gold in yore throat!
Hell's broke loose for forty miles aroun'
Bound to stop your music if yuh don't sing it down.]
Sing on the mountains, little whippoorwill,
Sing to the valleys, an' slap 'em with a hill,
For I'm struttin' high as an eagle's quill,
An' Hell's broke loose,
Hell's broke loose,
Hell's broke loose in Georgia!

They wasn't a sound when I stopped bowin'
(*Whippoorwill, yuh can sing no more.*)
But, somewhere or other, the dawn was growin',
(*Oh, mountain whippoorwill!*)

An' I thought, "I've fiddled all night an' lost.
Yo're a good hill-billy, but yuh've been bossed."

So I went to congratulate old man Dan,
—But he put his fiddle into my han'—
An' then the noise of the crowd began.

III. The Prairie

Comradeship exists between man and nature on the mountains, but rivalry exists between man and nature on the prairies. The cowboy struggles to control the range he wants for his home. And he is determined to succeed, despite nature's perpetual

mockery. The odds the cowboy defies are cried out by Lew
Sarett in "Breakers of Broncos": *

So! breakers of broncos! with miles of jagged wire,
You seek to break the spirit of this range;
With lariat of barbed wire fence, you hope
To tame its heart, and with your iron heel,
Hot from the desert, to sear upon its hip
Your molten brand—as wranglers at a round-up,
With bit and spur and lasso, strive to curb
And brand an outlaw fresh from winter range.

O breakers of broncos, listen! Can't you hear
The northwind snickering at you? the coyote
Upon the mesa, jeering? the waterfall
Chuckling among the rocks? the croaking magpie,
The hooting owl, the crane, the curlew? Look!
The chokecherry blossom, the sage, the bitter-root,
Bending with mirth wag their heads and laugh
At you! Why, even the broomtail cayuse kicks
His heels against the mountain sky, and snorts!

O breakers of broncos, we fling you on the wind
This handful of dust, this bitter alkali!—
As well attempt to rope the bucking stars,
Or burn your bars upon the flank of the moon!
When will you whirl your lasso at the sun?
Or bridle it? Or straddle the lightning-flash?

These are only three types of physical environment which are
home to different people—the city of the businessman, the mountain of the hillbilly, and the prairie of the cowboy.

Now let us turn to the spiritual hemisphere of man.

Wherever a man's home may be, as he becomes aware of its
beauties and its uglinesses, he begins to wonder, "What Infinite

* From *Slow Smoke*, by Lew Sarett. Copyright 1925 by Henry Holt and
Company, Inc.; copyright renewed 1953 by Lew Sarett. Reprinted by permission of Mrs. Lew Sarett.

originated this physical world—and me?" Some of the most famous
answers have been declared by Prophets, recorded as scriptures,
and practiced as religions, the bases of men's spiritual environments. Four concepts of God which affect millions of men are
Judaism, Mohammedanism, Buddhism, and Christianity.

A. Judaism

Those who accept Judaism believe in a god of justice. One
scripture which so describes him is Exodus 15. It contains the
song that Moses and the children of Israel sang unto their Lord
after He delivered them from slavery in Egypt.

[Then sang Moses and the children of Israel this song unto the
Lord, and spake, saying . . . ,] I will sing unto the LORD, for he
hath triumphed gloriously: the horse and his rider hath he thrown
into the sea.

The LORD *is* my strength and song, and he is become my salvation: he *is* my God, and I will prepare him a habitation; my
father's God, and I will exalt him.

[The LORD *is* a man of war: the LORD *is* his name.]

Pharaoh's chariots and his host hath he cast into the sea: [his
chosen captains also are drowned in the Red Sea.]

The depths have covered them: [they sank into the bottom as
a stone.]

Thy right hand, O LORD, is become glorious in power: thy right
hand, O LORD, hath dashed in pieces the enemy.

And in the greatness of thine excellency thou hast overthrown
them that rose up against thee: thou sentest forth thy wrath,
which consumed them as stubble.

And with the blast of thy nostrils the waters were gathered together, the floods stood upright as a heap, *and* the depths were
congealed in the heart of the sea.

[The enemy said, I will pursue, I will overtake, I will divide
the spoil; my lust shall be satisfied upon them; I will draw my
sword, my hand shall destroy them.

Thou didst blow with thy wind, the sea covered them, they sank
as lead in the mighty waters.]

Who *is* like unto thee, O LORD, among the gods? who *is* like
thee, glorious in holiness, fearful *in* praises, doing wonders?
Thou stretchedst out thy right hand, the earth swallowed them.
Thou in thy mercy hast led forth the people *which* thou hast
redeemed: thou hast guided *them* in thy strength unto thy holy
habitation.

[The people shall hear, and be afraid: sorrow shall take hold
on the inhabitants of Palestine.
Then the dukes of Edom shall be amazed; the mighty men of
Moab, trembling shall take hold upon them; all the inhabitants
of Canaan shall melt away.
Fear and dread shall fall upon them: by the greatness of thine
arm they shall be as still as a stone; till thy people pass over,
O LORD, till the people pass over, *which* thou hast purchased.]

Thou shalt bring them in, and plant them in the mountain of
thine inheritance, *in* the place, O LORD, *which* thou hast made for
thee to dwell in; *in* the sanctuary, O LORD, *which* thy hands have
established.
The LORD shall reign for ever and ever.

B. Mohammedanism

Whereas the Jewish God deals a justice that affects men's souls,
the Mohammedan God deals a justice that affects men's senses.
Passages throughout the *Koran* predict vividly the fleshly rewards
and punishments Allah gives.

God! There is no god but he; the Living, the Self-subsisting . . .
[neither slumber seizeth him, nor sleep;] his, whatsoever is in the
heavens and whatsoever is in the earth! [. . . Who is he that can
intercede with him but by his own permission?] He knoweth what is
present with his creatures, and what is yet to befall them; yet

naught of his knowledge do they comprehend, save what he
willeth . . .

When the sun shall be FOLDED UP,
And when the stars shall shoot downwards,
And when the mountains shall be set in motion,
[And when the camels ten months gone with foal shall be
    abandoned,
And when the wild beasts shall be gathered together,]
And when the seas shall be swollen,
[And when souls shall be paired with their bodies,
And when the damsel that had been buried alive shall be asked
For what crime she was put to death,
And when the leaves of the Book shall be unrolled,
And when the heaven shall be stripped away,]
And when hell shall be made to blaze,
And when paradise shall be brought near,
Every soul shall know what it hath produced . . .
    . . . And woe, on that day, to those who called the apostles liars,
[Who plunged for pastime into vain disputes]
On that day shall they be thrust with thrusting to the fire of hell:—
"This is the fire which ye treated as a lie!
[Is it magic, then? or, do ye not see it?]
Burn ye therein: and bear it patiently or impatiently it will be the
    same to you: [ye only receive the reward of your doings."]
But 'mid gardens and delights shall they dwell who have feared
    God,
[Rejoicing in what their Lord hath given them; and that from the
    pain of hell fire hath their Lord preserved them.
"Eat and drink with healthy enjoyment, in recompense for your
    deeds."]
On couches ranged in rows shall they recline; and to the damsels
    with large dark eyes will we wed them.
[And to those who have believed, whose offspring have followed
    them in the faith, will we again unite their offspring; nor of the

mood of their works will we in the least defraud them. Pledged
to God is every man for his actions.]
And fruits in abundance will we bestow on them, and such flesh
as they shall desire;
Therein shall they present to one another the cup which shall en-
gender no light discourse, no motive to sin:
[And youths shall go round unto them beautiful as imbedded
pearls:
And they shall accost one another and ask mutual questions.]
"A time indeed there was" will they say, "when we were full of
care as to the future lot of our families;
But kind hath God been to us, and from the pestilential torment
of the scorching wind hath he preserved us; . . .
("Ye only receive the reward of your doings.") *

C. Buddhism

Not all prophets believed the Infinite to be passionate. Buddha
believed the Supreme to be escape from feeling through perfect
thought. In *The Dhammapada* of Buddhist scripture is this explanation:

As a fletcher makes straight his arrow, a wise man makes
straight his trembling and unsteady thought, [which is difficult
to guard, difficult to hold back].

As a fish taken from his watery home and thrown on the dry
ground, our thought trembles all over in order to escape the
dominion of Mara, the tempter. It is good to tame the mind, which
is often difficult to hold in and flighty, [rushing wherever it listeth;]
a tamed mind brings happiness.

Let the wise man guard his thoughts, for they are difficult to
perceive, (and) very artful, [and they rush wherever they list:]
thoughts wellguarded bring happiness.

Before long, alas! this body will lie on the earth, despised,
without understanding, like a useless log.

* From *The Koran,* translated from the Arabic by J. M. Rodwell, London, Bernard Quaritch, 1876.

Whatever a hater may do to a hater, or an enemy to an enemy, a wrongly directed mind will do him greater mischief.

Not a mother, not a father, will do so much, nor any other relative; a well-directed mind will do us greater service.

All that we are is the result of what we have thought: it is founded on our thoughts, it is made up of our thoughts. If a man speaks or acts with an evil thought, pain follows him, as the wheel follows the foot of the ox that draws the carriage.

All that we are is the result of what we have thought: it is founded on our thoughts, it is made up of our thoughts. If a man speaks or acts with a pure thought, happiness follows him, like a shadow that never leaves him . . .*

D. Christianity

Christians also believe in an everlasting Supreme Being, but unlike the Buddhist god, He is more personal, like a loving father. Jesus' "Sermon on the Mount," recorded in St. Matthew,† tells of God's love.

Lay not up for yourselves treasures upon earth, where moth and rust doth corrupt, and where thieves break through and steal:

But lay up for yourselves treasures in heaven, where neither moth nor rust doth corrupt, and where thieves do not break through nor steal:

For where your treasure is, there will your heart be also.

[The light of the body is the eye: if therefore thine eye be single, thy whole body shall be full of light.

But if thine eye be evil, thy whole body shall be full of darkness. If therefore the light that is in thee be darkness, how great *is* that darkness!]

No man can serve two masters: for either he will hate the one,

* Lines from *The Dhammapada* from *Lectures on the Science of Religion with a Paper on Buddhist Nihilisn and a Translation of the Dhammapada or Path of Virtue* by Max Muller, M.A., New York, Charles Scribner's, 1872.

† St. Matthew, 6:19-34.

and love the other; or else he will hold to the one, and despise the other. Ye cannot serve God and Mammon.

Therefore I say unto you, Take no thought for your life, what ye shall eat, or what ye shall drink; nor yet for your body, what ye shall put on. Is not the life more than meat, and the body more than raiment?

Behold the fowls of the air; for they sow not, neither do they reap, nor gather into barns; yet your heavenly Father feedeth them. Are ye not much better than they?

[Which of you by taking thought can add one cubit unto his stature?

And why take ye thought for raiment?] (and) Consider the lilies of the field, how they grow; they toil not, neither do they spin;

And yet I say unto you, that even Solomon in all his glory was not arrayed like one of these.

Wherefore, if God so clothe the grass of the field, which today is, and tomorrow is cast into the oven, shall he not much more clothe you, [O ye of little faith?]

Therefore take no thought saying, What shall we eat, or, What shall we drink? or, Wherewithal shall we be clothed?

[(For after all these things do the Gentiles seek):] for your heavenly Father knoweth that ye have need of all these things.

But seek ye first the kingdom of God, and his righteousness; and all these things shall be added unto you.

Nightmare Sequence

RUTH DOUGHERTY

It's a funny thing about dreams—it's pretty easy to remember the good ones, and half the pleasure is in telling people about them. But it's hard to remember the nightmares—the details don't stay with you. Sometimes, though, nightmares leave you with the feeling that you should have remembered them—that maybe they would have meant something to you if you'd only written them down. Well, it was interesting to me to run across an author-poet who had nightmares like anyone else—and did something about them.

In one of his nightmares, Stephen Vincent Benét reflects the feeling that I'm sure all of us have had—that machines are becoming too human. Cars practically drive themselves. Unbelievable calculators solve our most intricate mathematical problems, and there are even machines that play chess and show signs of anger when they lose. The machine has almost become a living thing that dominates our lives; a thing by which we are enslaved more each day. Is it possible, then, that by some mischance they could take our world away from us? Could we become complete slaves to a machine-run society as Benét visualized in his almost too real . . . "Nightmare Number Three"? *

We had expected everything but revolt
And I kind of wonder myself when they started thinking—
But there's no dice in that now.

                              I've heard fellows say
They must have planned it for years and maybe they did.
Looking back, you can find little incidents here and there,
Like the concrete-mixer in Jersey eating the wop
Or the roto press that printed "Fiddle-dee-dee!"
In a three-color process all over Senator Sloop,
Just as he was making a speech. The thing about that
Was, how could it walk upstairs? But it was upstairs,
Clicking and mumbling in the Senate Chamber.
They had to knock out the wall to take it away
And the wrecking-crew said it grinned.

                              It was only the best
Machines, of course, the superhuman machines,
The ones we'd built to be better than flesh and bone,
But the cars were in it, of course . . .

                              and they hunted us

* From *Selected Works of Stephen Vincent Benét.* Holt, Rinehart & Winston, Inc. Copyright 1933, 1935, 1938 by Stephen Vincent Benét. Reprinted by permission of Brandt & Brandt.

Like rabbits through the cramped streets on that Bloody Monday,
The Madison Avenue busses leading the charge.
The busses were pretty bad—but I'll not forget
The smash of glass when the Duesenberg left the show-room
And pinned three brokers to the Racquet Club steps
Or the long howl of the horns when they saw men run,
When they saw them looking for holes in the solid ground . . .
I guess they were tired of being ridden in
And stopped and started by pygmies for silly ends,
Of wrapping cheap cigarettes and bad chocolate bars
Collecting nickels and waving platinum hair
And letting six million people live in a town.
I guess it was that. I guess they got tired of us
And the whole smell of human hands.

                                              But it was a shock
To climb sixteen flights of stairs to Art Zuckow's office
(Nobody took the elevators twice)
And find him strangled to death in a nest of telephones,
The octopus-tendrils waving over his head,
And a sort of quiet humming filling the air . . .
Do they eat? . . . There was red . . . But I did not stop to look.
I don't know yet how I got to the roof in time
And it's lonely, here on the roof.

                                      For a while, I thought
That window-cleaner would make it, and keep me company.
But they got him with his own hoist at the sixteenth floor
And dragged him in, with a squeal.
You see, they cooperate. Well, we taught them that
And it's fair enough, I suppose. You see, we built them.
We taught them to think for themselves.
It was bound to come. You can see it was bound to come.
And it won't be so bad, in the country. I hate to think
Of the reapers, running wild in the Kansas fields,
And the transport planes like hawks on a chickenyard,
But the horses might help. We might make a deal with the horses.

At least, you've more chance, out there.

                          And they need us, too.

They're bound to realize that when they once calm down.

They'll need oil and spare parts and adjustments and tuning up.

Slaves? Well, in a way, you know, we were slaves before.

There won't be so much real difference—honest, there won't.

(I wish I hadn't looked into that beauty-parlor

And seen what was happening there.

But those are female machines and a bit high-strung.)

Oh, we'll settle down. We'll arrange it. We'll compromise.

It wouldn't make sense to wipe out the whole human race.

Why, I bet if I went to my old Plymouth now

(Of course you'd have to do the tackful way)

And said, "Look here! Who got you the swell French horn?"

He wouldn't turn me over to those police cars;

At least I don't think he would.

                        Oh, it's going to be jake.

There won't be so much real difference—honest, there won't—

And I'd go down in a minute and take my chance—

I'm a good American and I always like them—

Except for one small detail that bothers me

And that's the food proposition. Because, you see,

The concrete-mixer may have made a mistake,

And it looks like just high spirits.

But, if it's got so they like the flavor—well—

And then there are the nightmares that overtake us on a hot night when sleep is hardly a reality. One might dream of the sun moving closer to the earth causing us to fall into a deep, tropic sleep. To further the nightmare, the lush jungle growth creeps into our minds as it would creep over the earth, bringing with it the unknown and frightening insects that thrive in steam heat. Even the already well known insects might take on new characteristics—they might feed differently, grow in size, or become more aggressive. A dream of swarms of huge locusts—frightening enough in their present state—might help you to understand the

frame of mind of Stephen Vincent Benét when he wrote his
"Metropolitan Nightmare." *

It rained quite a lot, that spring. You woke in the morning
And saw the sky still clouded, the streets still wet,
But nobody noticed so much, except the taxis
And the people who parade. You don't, in a city.
The parks got very green. All the trees were green
Far into July and August, heavy with leaf,
Heavy with leaf and the long roots boring and spreading,
But nobody noticed that but the city gardeners
And they don't talk.
     Oh, on Sundays, perhaps, you'd notice:
Walking through certain blocks, by the shut, proud houses
With the windows boarded, the people gone away,
You'd suddenly see the queerest small shoots of green
Poking through cracks and crevices in the stone
And a bird-sown flower, red on a balcony,
But then you made jokes about grass growing in the streets
And politics and grass-roots—and there were songs
And gags and a musical show called "Hot and Wet."
It all made a good box for the papers. When the flamingo
Flew into a meeting of the Board of Estimate,
The new Mayor acted at once and called the photographers.
When the first green creeper crawled upon Brooklyn Bridge,
They thought it was ornamental. They let it stay.
That was the year the termites came to New York
And they don't do well in cold climates—but listen, Joe,
They're only ants and ants are nothing but insects.
It was funny and yet rather wistful, in a way
(As Heywood Broun pointed out in the World-Telegram)
To think of them looking for wood in a steel city.
It made you feel about life. It was too divine.

 * From *Selected Works by Stephen Vincent Benét*. Holt, Rinehart &
Winston, Inc. Copyright 1933, 1935, 1938 by Stephen Vincent Benét. Reprinted by permission of Brandt & Brandt.

There were funny pictures by all the smart, funny artists
And Macy's ran a terribly clever ad:
"The Widow's Termite" or something.
                                    There was no
Disturbance. Even the Communists didn't protest
And say they were Morgan hirelings. It was too hot,
Too hot to protest, too hot to get excited,
An even, African heat, lush, fertile and steamy,
That soaked into bone and mind and never once broke.
The warm rain fell in fierce showers and ceased and fell.
Pretty soon you got used to its always being that way.

You got used to the changed rhythm, the altered beat,
To people walking slower, to the whole bright
Fierce pulse of the city slowing, to men in shorts,
To the new sun-helmets from Best's and the cops' white uniforms,
And the long noon-rest in the offices, everywhere.
It wasn't a plan or anything. It just happened.
The fingers tapped the keys slower, the office-boys
Dozed on their benches, the bookkeeper yawned at his desk.
The A. T. & T. was the first to change the shifts
And establish an official siesta-room,
But they were always efficient. Mostly it just
Happened like sleep itself, like a tropic sleep,
Till even the Thirties were deserted at noon
Except for a few tourists and one damp cop.
They ran boats to see the big lilies on the North River
But it was only the tourists who really noticed
The flocks of rose-and-green parrots and parakeets
Nesting in the stone crannies of the Cathedral.
The rest of us had forgotten when they first came.

There wasn't any real change, it was just a heat spell,
A rain spell, a funny summer, a weather-man's joke,
In spite of the geraniums three feet high
In the tin-gardens of Hester and Desbrosses.

New York was New York. It couldn't turn inside out.
When they got the news from Woods Hole about the Gulf Stream,
The Times ran an adequate story.
But nobody reads those stories but science-cranks.

Until, one day, a somnolent city-editor
Gave a new cub the termite yarn to break his teeth on.
The cub was just down from Vermont, so he took the time.
He was serious about it. He went around.
He read all about termites in the Public Library
And it made him sore when they fired him.

                                    So, one evening,
Talking with an old watchman, beside the first
Raw girders of the new Planetopolis Building
(Ten thousand brine-cooled offices, each with shower)
He saw a dark line creeping across the rubble
And turned a flashlight on it.
                              "Say, buddy," he said,
"You better look out for those ants. They eat wood, you know,
They'll have your shack down in no time."
                                    The watchman spat.
"Oh, they've quit eating wood," he said, in a casual voice,
"I thought everybody knew that."
                              —and reaching down,
He pried from the insect jaws the bright crumb of steel.

    Benét had one nightmare that haunts me more than his others.
Maybe it's because of its pertinency to our own times—the crying
out against war and what it might do to us. Poets and philosophers
have always written of possible solutions to the problem of war
and how to stop it. Even in the fifth century B.C., Aristophanes
wrote his comedy *Lysistrata* as a mock solution to the war problem. He seemed to feel that the power of stopping wars could well
be in the hands of the women, and although Benét's "Nightmare
for Future Reference" handles the matter in an entirely different
way, he also believes that women can smash the war machine.
His is a nightmare that is almost shockingly real in our present

day—one that might well be kept on hand . . . a "Nightmare
for Future Reference." *

That was the second year of the Third World War,
The one between Us and Them.
                                        Well we've gotten used.
We don't talk much about it, queerly enough.
There was all sorts of talk the first years after the Peace,
A million theories, a million wild suppositions,
A million hopeful explanations and plans,
But we don't talk about it now. We don't even ask.
We might do the wrong thing. I don't guess you'd understand that.
But you're eighteen, now. You can take it. You'd better know.

You see, you were born just before the war broke out.
Who started it? Oh, they said it was Us or Them
And it looked like it at the time. You don't know what that's like.
But anyhow, it started and there it was,
Just a little worse, of course, than the one before,
But mankind was used to that. We didn't take notice.
They bombed our capital and we bombed theirs.
You've been to the Broken Towns? Yes, they take you there.
They show you the look of the tormented earth.
But They can't show the smell of the gas or the death
Or how it felt to be there, and a part of it.
But we didn't know. I swear that we didn't know.

I remember the first faint hint there was something wrong,
Something beyond all wars and bigger and strange,
Something you couldn't explain.
                                        I was back on leave—
Strange, as you felt on leave, as you always felt—
But I went to see the Chief at the hospital
And there he was, in the same old laboratory,

* From *Selected Works of Stephen Vincent Benét*. Holt, Rinehart &
Winston, Inc. Copyright 1933, 1935, 1938 by Stephen Vincent Benét. Reprinted by permission of Brandt & Brandt.

A little older, with some white in his hair
But the same eyes that went through you and the same tongue.
They hadn't been able to touch him—not the bombs
Nor the ruin of his life's work nor anything.
He blinked at me from behind his spectacles
And said, "Huh. It's you. They won't let me have guinea pigs
Except for the war work, but I steal a few.
And they've made me a colonel—expect me to salute.
Damn fools. A damn-fool business. I don't know how.
Have you heard what Erickson's done with the ductless glands?
The journals are four months late. Sit down and smoke."
And I did and it was like home.
                          He was a great man.
You might remember that—and I'd worked with him.
Well, finally he said to me, "How's your boy?"
"Oh—healthy," I said. "We're lucky."
                          "Yes," he said,
And a frown went over his face. "He might even grow up,
Though the intervals between wars are getting shorter.
I wonder if it wouldn't simplify things
To declare mankind in a permanent state of siege.
It might knock some sense in their heads."
                          "You're cheerful,"
  I said.
"Oh, I'm always cheerful," he said. "Seen these, by the way?"
He tapped some charts on a table.
                          "Seen what?" I said.
"Oh," he said, with that devilish, sidelong grin of his,
"Just the normal city statistics—death and birth.
You're a soldier now. You wouldn't be interested.
But the birth rate's dropping—"
                          "Well, really, sir," I said,
We know that it's always dropped, in every war."

"Not like this," he said. "I can show you the curve.
It looks like the side of a mountain, going down.

And faster, the last three months—yes, a good deal faster.
I showed it to Lobenheim and he was puzzled.
It makes a neat problem—yes?" He looked at me.

"They'd better make peace," he said. "They'd better make peace."

"Well, sir," I said, "if we break through, in the spring . . ."
"Break through?" he said. "What's that? They'd better make peace.
The stars may be tired of us. No, I'm not a mystic.
I leave that to the big scientists in bad novels.
But I never saw such a queer maternity curve.
I wish I could get to Ehrens, on their side.
He'd tell me the truth. But the fools won't let me do it."

His eyes looked tired as he stared at the careful charts.
"Suppose there are no more babies?" he said. "What then?
It's one way of solving the problem."
                                        "But, sir—" I said.
"But, sir!" he said. "Will you tell me, please, what is life?
Why it's given, why it's taken away?
Oh, I know—we make a jelly inside a test tube,
We keep a cock's heart living inside a jar.
We know a great many things and what do we know?
We think we know what finished the dinosaurs
But do we? Maybe they were given a chance
And then it was taken back. There are other beasts
That only kill for their food. No, I'm not a mystic,
But there's a certain pattern in nature, you know,
And we're upsetting it daily. Eat and mate
And go back to the earth after that, and that's all right,
But now we're blasting and sickening earth itself.
She's been very patient with us. I wonder how long."

Well, I thought the Chief had gone crazy, just at first,
And then I remembered the look of no man's land,
That bitter landscape, pockmarked like the moon,

Lifeless as the moon's face and horrible,
The thing we'd made with the guns.

                            If it were earth,
It looked as though it hated.

                  "Well?" I said,
And my voice was a little thin. He looked hard at me.
"Oh—ask the women," he grunted. "Don't ask me.
Ask them what they think about it."

                        I didn't ask them,
Not even your mother—she was strange, those days—
But, two weeks later, I was back in the lines
And somebody sent me a paper—
Encouragement for the troops and all of that—
All about the fall of Their birth rate on Their side.

I guess you know, now. There was still a day when we fought
And the next day, the women knew. I don't know how they knew,
But they smashed every government in the world
Like a heap of broken china, within two days,
And we'd stopped firing by then. And we looked at each other.

We didn't talk much, those first weeks. You couldn't talk.
We started in rebuilding and that was all,
And at first, nobody would even touch the guns,
Not even to melt them up. They just stood there, silent,
Pointing the way they had and nobody there.
And there was a kind of madness in the air,
A quiet, bewildered madness, strange and shy.
You'd pass a man who was muttering to himself
And you'd know what he was muttering, and why.
I remember coming home and your mother there.
She looked at me, at first didn't speak at all,
And then she said, "Burn those clothes. Take them off and burn
   them
Or I'll never touch you or speak to you again."
And then I knew I was still in my uniform.

Well, I've told you, now. They tell you now at eighteen.
There's no use telling before.
                          Do you understand?
That's why we have the Ritual of the Earth,
The Day of Sorrow, the other ceremonies.
Oh yes, at first people hated the animals
Because they still bred, but we've gotten over that.
Perhaps they can work it better, when it's their turn,
If it's their turn—I don't know. I don't know at all.
You can call it a virus, of course, if you like the word,
But we haven't been able to find it. Not yet. No.
It isn't as if it had happened all at once.
There were a few children born in the last six months
Before the end of the war, so there's still some hope.
But they're almost grown. That's the trouble. They're almost
    grown.
Well, we had a long run. That's something. At first they thought
There might be a nation somewhere—a savage tribe.
But we were all in it, even the Eskimos,
And we keep the toys in the stores, and the colored books,
And people marry and plan and the rest of it,
But, you see, there aren't any children. They aren't born.

The Value of Life: As the Pessimist Sees It

STERLING NORRIS

Seen down the perspective of the centuries, the history of man's
moral evaluation of the world and life appears as a panorama of
light and dark. Thus it is generally agreed that the Age of Pericles,
its ugly features dimmed by time, was a dynamic period of idealism
and order, a glorious age of the affirmation of reason and beauty;
that the Middle Ages was a time whose apparent negation of this
life is perhaps too easily symbolized by the popular theme of the
Dance of Death; that the Renaissance, beginning in fourteenth-

century Italy and extending through the spacious times of great Elizabeth, was an era of abundant vitality; and that this age was followed by others in which man's thinking seems to have been dominantly pessimistic or optimistic in tone down to our own age of bewildering revelation and disillusionment. The very terms "Dark Ages," "Renaissance," and "Age of Doubt" signify in themselves that men and civilizations were dominated (as it seems to us) by the conviction that life in itself was "stale, flat, and unprofitable," or knew a resurgence of belief in the value of life rather than the darkness of uncertainty.

It is to this varying response to life that men commonly refer when they speak of their philosophy. To some degree everyone exemplifies one or the other of these attitudes: he is primarily an optimist or a pessimist. My recital presents variations of the pessimistic view.

My first selection, from *Candide,* shows the conflict between these two diverse evaluations of life. *Candide* as a whole was written to repudiate Leibnitz's doctrine of pre-established harmony, the theory that all the universe is a result of wise design, that this is the best of all possible worlds. Voltaire insists that this view will not meet the test of practical experience: evil is a fact, not an illusion; worst of all, men are by nature conditioned to evil.

What Happened to Candide and Martin in France

Then, turning to him, [Candide] said:

"Sir, no doubt you think that all is for the best in the physical world and in the moral, and that nothing could be otherwise than as it is?"

"Sir," replied the man of letters, "I do not think anything of the sort. I think everything goes awry with us, that nobody knows his rank or his office, nor what he is doing, nor what he ought to do, and that except at supper, which is quite gay and where there appears to be a certain amount of sociability, all the rest of their time is passed in senseless quarrels: Lawyers with churchmen, men of letters with men of letters, courtiers with courtiers, financiers with the people, wives with husbands, relatives with relatives; 'tis an eternal war."

Candide replied:

"I have seen worse things; but a wise man, who has since had the misfortune to be hanged, taught me that it is all for the best; these are only the shadows in a fair picture."

"Your wise man who was hanged was poking fun at the world," said Martin; "and your shadows are horrible stains."

"The stains are made by men," said Candide, "and they cannot avoid them."

"Then it is not their fault," said Martin.

Pessimism may manifest itself in a variety of ways, but it is usually a disillusionment with life or religion. Sometimes this disillusionment may be an individual uneasiness, a lack of personal adjustment to one's time and circumstances. Yet the main reason why we approve of Wordsworth's sonnet, "The World Is Too Much with Us," is that it expresses the oppression that we all feel in our too complex world.

The World Is Too Much with Us

WILLIAM WORDSWORTH

The world is too much with us; late and soon,
Getting and spending, we lay waste our powers:
Little we see in Nature that is ours;
We have given our hearts away, a sordid boon!
This Sea that bares her bosom to the moon;
The winds that will be howling at all hours,
And are up-gathered now like sleeping flowers;
For this, for everything, we are out of tune;
It moves us not.—Great God! I'd rather be
A Pagan suckled in a creed outworn;
So might I, standing on this pleasant lea,
Have glimpses that would make me less forlorn;
Have sight of Proteus rising from the sea;
Or hear old Triton blow his wreathèd horn.

This almost unrelieved gloom, which is made blacker to us by our own modern misgivings about our civilization, has its ancient parallel in the words of the Preacher, whose admonition has long sobered the thoughtful:

From Ecclesiastes; or The Preacher

The words of the Preacher, the son of David, king in Jerusalem.

Vanity of vanities, sai*th* the Preacher, vanity of vanities; all is vanity.

What profit hath a man of all his labor which he taketh under the sun?

One generation passeth away, and another generation cometh; but the earth abideth for ever.

The sun also ariseth, and the sun goeth down, and hasteth to his place where he arose.

The wind goeth toward the south, and turneth about unto the north; it whirleth about continually, and the wind returneth again according to his circuits.

All the rivers run into the sea; yet the sea is not full; unto the place from whence the rivers come, thither they return again.

All things are full of labor; man cannot utter it: the eye is not satisfied with seeing, nor the ear filled with hearing.

The thing that hath been, it is that which shall be; and that which is done is that which shall be done; and there is no new thing under the sun.

Is there any thing whereof it may be said, See, this is new? it hath been already of old time, which was before us.

There is no remembrance of former things; neither shall there be any remembrance of things that are to come with those that shall come after.

I the Preacher was king over Israel in Jerusalem.

And I gave my heart to seek and search out by wisdom concerning all things that are done under heaven: this sore travail hath God given to the sons of man to be exercised therewith.

I have seen all the works that are done under the sun; and, behold, all is vanity and vexation of spirit.

One encounters the theme of the vanity and painful futility of human affairs in poetry and philosophy everywhere. In the defeat of the pretensions of a tyrant "Ozymandias," one may take a gloomy pleasure, but the larger application of the idea leaves little comfort.

Ozymandias

PERCY BYSSHE SHELLEY

I met a traveler from an antique land
Who said: Two vast and trunkless legs of stone
Stand in the desert. Near them, on the sand,
Half sunk, a shattered visage lies, whose frown,
And wrinkled lip, and sneer of cold command,
Tell that the sculptor well those passions read
Which yet survive, stamped on these lifeless things,
The hand that mocked them and the heart that fed;
And on the pedestal these words appear:
"My name is Ozymandias, king of kings:
Look on my works, ye Mighty, and despair!"
Nothing beside remains. Round the decay
Of that colossal wreck, boundless and bare
The lone and level sands stretch far away.

Worse than the vanity and painful futility of human affairs is the desolation that comes from the loss of one's ideals. To most people, as to Philip Carey in *Of Human Bondage,* dark moments come when all that they have been taught to revere seems false.

. . . He did not know how wide a country, arid and precipitous, must be crossed before the traveler through life comes to an acceptance of reality. It is an illusion that youth is happy, an illusion of those who have lost it; but the young know they are wretched, for they are full of the truthless ideals which have been instilled into them, and each time they come in contact with the real they are bruised and wounded. It looks as if they were victims of a conspiracy; for the books they read, ideal by the necessity of selection, and the conversation of their elders who look back upon the past through a rosy haze of forgetfulness, prepare them for an unreal life. They must discover for themselves that all they have read and all they have been told are lies, lies, lies; and each discovery is another nail driven into the body on the cross of life. The strange thing is that each one who has gone through that bitter disillusionment adds to it in his turn, unconsciously by the power within him which is stronger than himself. The companionship of Hayward was the worst possible thing for Philip. He was a man who was nothing for himself, but only through a literary atmosphere, and he was dangerous because he had deceived himself into sincerity. He honestly mistook his sensuality for romantic emotion, his vacillation for the artistic temperament, and his idleness for philosophic calm. His mind, vulgar in its effort at refinement, saw everything a little larger than life size, with the outlines blurred, in a golden mist of sentimentality. He lied and never knew that he lied, and when it was pointed out to him said that lies were beautiful. He was an idealist.*

If life is nothing but vanity, painful futility and desolation, why do we not consider death? Why not commit suicide?

This escape of despair is rejected by Hamlet on supernatural grounds—the "dread of something after death."

Hamlet, 111, i

HAMLET:

    To be, or not to be: that is the question:

    Whether 'tis nobler in the mind to suffer

* From *Of Human Bondage* by W. Somerset Maugham. Copyright 1917 by George H. Doran Company. Reprinted by permission of Doubleday and Company, Inc., and of W. Somerset Maugham and Heinemann Ltd.

The slings and arrows of outrageous fortune,
Or to take arms against a sea of troubles,
And by opposing end them. To die: to sleep;
No more: and, by a sleep to say we end
The heart-ache and the thousand natural shocks
That flesh is heir to, 'tis a consummation
Devoutly to be wished. To die, to sleep;
To sleep; perchance to dream: ay, there's the rub;
For in that sleep of death what dreams may come
When we have shuffled off this mortal coil,
Must give us pause. There's the respect
That makes calamity of so long life;
For who would bear the whips and scorns of time,
The oppressor's wrong, the proud man's contumely,
The pangs of despised love, the law's delay,
The insolence of office and the spurns
That patient merit of the unworthy takes,
When he himself might his quietus make
With a bare bodkin? who would these fardels bear,
To grunt and sweat under a weary life,
But that the dread of something after death,
The undiscovered country from whose bourn
No traveler returns, puzzles the will,
And makes us rather bear those ills we have
Than fly to others that we know not of?
Thus conscience does make cowards of us all;
And thus the native hue of resolution
Is sicklied o'er with the pale cast of thought,
And enterprises of great pith and moment
With this regard their currents turn awry,
And lose the name of action.

If ours is a hostile universe and we find it difficult to cope with, perhaps we can still find solace in human love as expressed in the noble mind of Matthew Arnold.

Dover Beach

MATTHEW ARNOLD

The sea is calm tonight.
The tide is full, the moon lies fair
Upon the straits:—on the French coast, the light
Gleams, and is gone; the cliffs of England stand,
Glimmering and vast, out in the tranquil bay.
Come to the window, sweet is the night-air!
Only, from the long line of spray
Where the sea meets the moon-blanched land,
Listen! you hear the grating roar
Of pebbles which the waves draw back, and fling,
At their return, up the high strand,
Begin, and cease, and then again begin,
With tremulous cadence slow, and bring
The eternal note of sadness in.

Sophocles long ago
Heard it on the Aegean, and it brought
Into his mind the turbid ebb and flow
Of human misery; we
Find also in the sound a thought,
Hearing it by this distant northern sea.

The Sea of Faith
Was once, too, at the full, and round earth's shore
Lay like the folds of a bright girdle furled;
But now I only hear
Its melancholy, long, withdrawing roar,
Retreating, to the breath
Of the night-wind, down the vast edges drear
And naked shingles of the world.
Ah, love, let us be true
To one another! for the world, which seems

To lie before us like a land of dreams,
So various, so beautiful, so new,
Hath really neither joy, nor love, nor light,
Nor certitude, nor peace, nor help for pain;
And we are here as on a darkling plain
Swept with confused alarms of struggle and flight,
Where ignorant armies clash by night.

Perhaps it could be said, finally, that the pessimistic view in its best aspects is not ignoble. There is an untarnished glory in the dark view of life.